"MAMA SOU"

"Mama Sou"
Now You See Him - Now You Don't

Maria Griggs & Tyler Clapp

This is a work of fiction based on true events. All character names, except for the protagonist, have been changed. Locations and dialogue in this novel are based on true events and described based on my recollection of them.

© 2019 Maria Griggs & Tyler Clapp. All rights reserved.
ISBN - 9781645503736

No part of this book may be reproduced, stored in a retrieval system, or transmitted by any means without the written permission of the author.

Any people depicted in stock imagery provided by Thinkstock are models, and such images are being used for illustrative purposes only.
Certain stock imagery © Thinkstock.

This book is printed on acid-free paper.

Because of the dynamic nature of the Internet, any web addresses or links contained in this book may have changed since publication and may no longer be valid. The views expressed in this work are solely those of the author and do not necessarily reflect the views of the publisher, and the publisher hereby disclaims any responsibility for them.

Images and Graphics by Brandon Griggs

Epigraph

"I shall be telling this with a sigh
Somewhere ages and ages hence:
Two roads diverged in a wood, and I—
I took the one less traveled by,
And that has made all the difference."

–Robert Frost, "*The Road Not Taken*"

"And one has to understand that braveness is not the absence of fear but rather the strength to keep on going forward despite the fear."

–Paulo Coelho

DEDICATION

To my son George. I hope you now know a little more than you knew before . . .

I also would like to dedicate this book to all parents who, at some time or another, were forced to make a decision of great magnitude that was to affect, not only themselves, but someone else whom they loved wholeheartedly and unconditionally: Their child.

MARIA GRIGGS

Dedicated to my father, who let me pursue authorhood despite his misgivings. You are my inspiration, the kind of person I want to be.

TYLER CLAPP

Foreword

This book was almost never finished.

Maria came to me with her story, said she enjoyed my writing style from the stories I had posted online and wanted me to help put her tale to paper. She had me intrigued, the story was interesting and it was a good chance to expand my horizons outside of genre fiction. After a little negotiating, we had an arrangement, and the work began to turn her experiences into a piece of writing we could both be proud of.

I got a few pages in before I started feeling angry for no reason at all. It wasn't a particular passage that had set me off, if was what was going to happen in the story. The early stages of the book went mostly unhindered by this simmering emotion, but later into the endeavor it became too much to bear.

I began putting off the project, finding personal excuses as to why I could not do it now, but deep down I knew I feared that anger. Irrational, clawing, seething rage was starting to spill into the rest of my life, dragging others into the maelstrom of inexplicable and unquenchable ire.

It was not any inability; the words were practically there, I just needed to put them down. It was not any legal trouble, any personal issues, any conflicting schedules. All that stood in my way was a mire of fury that blinded me from my creative vision.

This book should not have ever happened. This story should never have to be told. For all my years as a writer, I never came upon a story I did not want to tell, until I started this one. The fact that the "official" story was nowhere near the truth made it that much more unbearable. What happened to Maria was something that no one should ever have to suffer; writing it all down made it far too real for me.

I was ready to quit. I had just about made up my mind, and told my roommate, Maria's youngest son, as much. I was in no condition to finish this, I thought myself a poor excuse for a writer, too scared of the story to even try to tell it.

He told me try again, to sit with it one more time. If I could hold on and push through, it would be a fantastic opportunity to make my name in the world of literature, and possibly the only chance Maria had at getting her story told.

I sat working on it once more, trying to reconcile my wrath. Driven to distraction by my silent outrage, it began to dawn on me that this was exactly how Maria must have felt, must still feel, all this time. The only way this vexation would be cured for both of us would be to bring the truth to light, have everyone read our story — and it was ours now — and know what really happened to her.

I could not give her that time back. But in at least one small way, I could give her justice.

Rage became passion, and once again I put my hands to the keys. I could not give up now; not when she needed me the most.

This book would never have happened in a perfect world. But our world is far from perfect, even in our dreams. This story is the culmination of joy, rage, sorrow, passion, justice, and the pursuit of happiness of one person condensed into five parts. Know as you read it that you give us solace, and play a part in the healing that started when Maria first came to me with a story to tell.

Read these words, and spread them like wildfire. It is the least she deserves.

TYLER CLAPP

Foreword II

Between lies and truth, there is a gap. This gap was my life for 40 years. I cannot know for sure what is *truth* and what are *lies*, but this book represents to me the *missing half* of my story — the other half is my life as a child.

Unfortunately, I can't say if this *gap* will ever close… The lies and truths I have experienced changed my life forever, but also made me very strong! That is the reason I always keep walking. Slow but safe. Always with the truth by me. With a conscious commitment to be a better person every day.

We live once! So, why not live as a good person? Don't let anyone make you show the world your "bad face" and live that way. Be loyal to your true self with no consequences to anyone!

So, take care of yourself and try to be a better person every day!

GIORGOS ALKAIOS

Introduction

Imagine, if you don't mind, being a parent. For some this should be quite simple as you are parents and therefore this is a simple exercise where there is no use for rhetoric — you may fill in the faces of your wife or husband, the faces of your children, into these theoretical characters. But for those, like myself who are only sons and daughters (not even wife or husband), humor me for a moment and try to put yourself into this position.

Christmas mornings, your young son awakens and trots down the stairs just after you finish loading the last of "Santa's" presents into his stocking. Maybe you just finished wrapping that one toy he told you he hoped that Santa would know he *really* wanted. It's early, too early to be awake, and your little guy is NEVER awake this early — never except on Christmas Day. You sit down, dressed in your finest 14 dollar robe from Kmart, sipping on coffee because you lie and tell him you are tired and "need the caffeine", in reality you are almost as excited as he is to watch the unveiling of the presents before him. It's one of those days that as a parent you know you're child will feel nothing but warmth and happiness and joy, not just because of the presents but because you see him years from now doing the same thing you are doing for your grandchildren. You know this will be a day that he will come to remember for years. You are in turn creating moments of joy he will create for his children, who will create for his children, and so on . . . what the hell do you really need a cup of coffee for when you have a son on Christmas?

Stay a bit longer on another example. Your child is now 12 years old, dressed in black pants, black dress belt (like his Dad wears to work), black dress shoes that are too big for him but he doesn't realize because he just slips the shoes on without unknotting them, and that crisp white shirt that you help him button all the way up before putting on a junior sized tie that makes him really look like a miniature model of his father. He struts around, looking somewhat awkward with his oversized shoes and a button up shirt that itches his neck, but regardless he *struts.* He walks around the house feeling older and displaying the air of a boy who isn't 12, but almost a teenager! He will be performing tonight. With 29 classmates in a gymnasium that, to him, will feel like the Metropolitan Opera House when his voice hits the high notes of "Circle of Life" from the Lion King movie in his schools production of *Disney Classics!* You will be sitting somewhere in the middle of the audience, on a hard steel folding chair, camera in one hand, smile upon your face, and with the other hand holding the hand of the partner who one time looked into your eyes and said, "We're having a boy." He will try to act like a professional, but when the song is over, his eyes will scour the audience looking for you and will make a small gesture to know he found you—"Hi Mom."

I know I have taken too much time, but I promise you I am getting the reason for this exercise shortly . . . my last scenario involved your son sitting in his room, quietly. By this point in parenthood you know with the confidence of a 16 year veteran of war, that something is wrong—no son of yours is *ever* quiet in his room. Dinner is microwaved up, and ready to be consumed in the mad dash through the house that you're young adult usually finds himself in every night on his way out to his friend so-and-so's house, or the something-or-other mall, or to go see the movie what's-it-called. But tonight it's quiet. Pavlov would have guaranteed that a simple *Ding!* From your microwave would have brought him down the stairs, but he would have been wrong. As you enter the room, he is sitting on his bed, music playing into a set of headphones he has one, with two thumbs on his cell phone (I don't think that cell phones and a teenagers hand will ever lose their connection in the next millennia to come). As you sit down on the corner of his bed and look around the room at the posters of athletes, rock stars, women, whatever that is important to a 16 year old, he looks up at you. He then does what every parent will understand—he will roll his eyes and turn to look away from you. You will have to play this one just right, and place your hand on his knee, don't rub his head that's for little kids, and look at him. As a strong young man, he will look at you and remind you of the boy who opened Christmas presents. His eyes will water-up, and he will tell you that the love of his life has moved on to someone else. He won't know how life is supposed to move forward, nor how to show his face at school. He doesn't know how people are supposed to feel this bad and just... live. But you do. And in this moment you tell him a story of your first love, and how it wasn't his mother, but "Jenny" from Spanish class! The two of you will laugh, cry a bit, and he will come downstairs and for the first time since he was 13 — he will sit at the table and eat dinner with you and talk about who he is, and what he did today.

Hopefully, I have painted a picture of the upbringing you're child deserves. Hopefully, without realizing, you have smiled in regards to the life you hope you too may have, as a parent. Hopefully, you have visualized these scenes and felt warmth. Hopefully, colors were so rich and defined, the purest of whites and yellows. Hopefully, at no point, did you question what you know, logically speaking, happens in life. The innocent perception of life found in children eventually darkens, becomes blurred, and the moments of warmth are shelters found in a landscape of cold and icy reality. We know this, and we realize our children will come to understand the balance of warmth and cold, light and dark, clear and blurred *over time and pray it hits once they are given the tools necessary to survive and thrive in all conditions.*

Now, it is my apologies to darken the setting of these pictures of Rockwellesque parental joys, but in turn see your son on Christmas without you. See your son singing to an empty seat. See your son left wondering why love didn't last. See yourself thousands of miles away, and knowing where he is, and not being able to do a damn thing about it. See yourself every day waking up and knowing your son has gone another day without you, and those days are becoming closer and closer to the amount of days he had with you. Your son is growing up becoming more accustom to life without you, than with you.

For Maria, her life was full of strong family, friends, hopes, dreams, and love. True love. Young love. On a warm Boston day, Maria's balmy summer life was to be placed on a collision course with the most frigid, most unwelcoming, and harshest of storms that could destroy a young girl's soul. There was no way for her to expect what was to come, and no way for her to have been prepared for the depth of cold she was to feel. Just as any person who has never seen a blizzard, you never know how cold and windy it will get until it shows up.

The question comes, "What does one do when they have realized life can be cold?"

The answer is "Find warmth. Anywhere. Any way. Just get warm."

For Maria, this is the story of her cold winters, where others may have given up and succumb to the cold, she found a spark of hope to give her just enough to live her life, without ever forgetting about the child who was stolen from her. Her struggle against politics, the law, the man who betrayed her, and anyone trying to put out her small bit of hope.

Acknowledgements

There are so many people that I need to acknowledge, but I must start with the ones directly involved with this work:

Tyler Clapp: Your writing style was the push I needed to approach you with my idea—You did an excellent job! I hope we can work together again on a future project . . . you are invaluable!

Michael Griggs, Manager, Publicist, Public Relations, Marketing Consultant, sounding board, "Go To" guy, and a wonderful son. Couldn't have managed without you!

Lucia Robinson-Griggs, Editor and idea-vault. Thank you for your feedback and input, your mind gave me the key to a perfect ending!

Adam Griggs, who took time out of his very hectic schedule on the football field to do an amazing job on the Introduction and various other matter for this book—I still choke up when I read it . . . . Thank you for agreeing to contribute, you're my rock!

Brandon Griggs, never hesitated to dig deeper into his imagination in order to get the image from my mind's eye and make it a reality. Thanks for your inquisitiveness and brilliance!

My husband, Terry, for his unwavering support and consistent effort to "keep us afloat" while I was working on our business, this emotion-driven project, and traveling all over the East Coast. You *"kept the lights on"*! . . . And to the many friends and family members who—even though thought it may be a process too painful to relive—supported my idea and encouraged me every step of the way. Thank you!

PART I

INNOCENCE AND THE BLESSINGS OF FAMILY

Maria thought of marriage as a blessing. It was a beautiful union of two souls in love, the ultimate celebration of two lives. It was a joining deep within the soul, and the more time spent so entwined could only be a greater blessing. It was only natural to be complete with another person, to open her heart and give all her love to that person. There was no other way it could be; for her it was the only possibility.

Marko and she had been together for several months and he had seen this belief in her. He was her first love, and the time was right. Maybe this is why when Marko proposed to her, she said yes. It was the only thing she could ever have said, especially to him. There could have been no other answer, because marriage was a blessing, and Maria loved him so very much. It never occurred to her that she could have waited, or said no, because it was only natural to get married.

After a short visit from Marko's father, where he blessed their upcoming union, the marriage took place in a small island off the coast of Piraeus, Salamis. For their honeymoon, Marko brought her to the island of Rhodes. Maria had read about this island and loved the city; its history, its architecture, and the beautiful harbor were a delight to the seventeen year old Portuguese girl. She and Marko traveled all over the island to see the big attractions: The Grand Master's Palace, Knight's Street, the Acropolis of Rhodes, and many more, but what stood out to Maria was the famous Colossus of Rhodes. Of course, the statue had been destroyed long ago, but the site where it once stood was still a place of great fame.

As she stood against the stone wall, her head cupped in her hands as she peered over the harbor, Marko told her about the story of the Colossus. He told her how the people used to believe the Colossus was the protector of the port, and how it fell to the waters below.

"That's amazing," Maria said.

"It's still there," Marko said. "All the pieces are down in the water, even to this day. No one wants to get the pieces to put it back together. They leave it there to pay homage to the memory of what happened."

Maria turned to the water, trying to picture it all. She imagined dreamily that the Colossus below the water still protected its people to this day, even while they refused to rebuild it.

"Why would the people just leave their guardian at the bottom of the harbor like that?" Maria wondered aloud while she watched the harbor. She did not like leaving problems lying around, and wanted to fix things if she could. Where there was a will, there was a way, and there must have been a will somewhere to get the Colossus fixed. "It was something special, something they once had so much love for. They believed the Colossus protected them, why would the ancient Greeks want to leave it at the bottom of the sea?"

"Fear," Marko told her. "They were afraid they had angered the gods with their guardian. When they were offered to have it rebuilt, they refused, all because they feared divine consequences."

"So they just abandoned their beloved giant just like that? All to make the gods happy?" she asked.

Marko nodded. "Small price to pay for peace of mind, I'd say."

How foolish, Maria thought. Isn't any cost worth saving something you love?

But no, it occurred to Maria that that was not always true. She herself knew that sometimes fate had a way of guiding you toward what you were meant for, even if it meant taking you from something that could have been special. That was how Maria met Marko in the first place.

♑♓♑♓♑♓♑♓♑♓♑♓

It happened when she moved to America, while she was still in high school. It was the last few days of summer school, at the tail end of a beautifully warm season. Maria was not doing poorly in school, far from it. Her old school in Caracas was an experimental school that attempted to compress 6 years of education into 4. By her tenth year of school, she had the equivalent of 12 years under her cap. However, when she came to America with her family, she was placed in tenth grade because of her age, and later into a school for immigrants, the focus of which was on English pronunciation and grammar.

Her commute to the summer school in Jamaica Plains was quite the trek. She went from a long bus ride that started in Brighton, Massachusetts where she lived, then a street car to yet another bus ride that finally landed her in Jamaica Plains. It was an hour there and an hour back every day, a long commute to make especially for a girl in high school.

But Maria never let the long trek defeat her. She took it as an adventure, just another part of her learning experience, to be taken in and absorbed like any other lesson. She even started leaving early, so she could take more time to see what there was to see. In no time, she found that the school was only blocks away from Jamaica Pond, a beautiful pond that she could stop at on hot days to cool off for a while before continuing on her way to school.

One particularly warm day, right near the end of summer school, while she was dipping her feet into this pool, she heard someone come up behind her.

"How's the water?"

She turned to see a young man, in his very early twenties, wearing jogging clothes standing behind her. He looked as though he had been exercising for quite some time, slightly out of breath and perspiring from the hot sun.

"Oh, it's fine," she said politely. "It's nice and cool."

"Do you mind if I join you?" he asked.

Maria waved to the pond, indicating that she did not mind, and he proceeded to sit next to her, take off his socks and shoes and join her.

They both talked for a while, just enjoying this lovely pond on a warm day, and he introduced himself as Matt. He was in college, actually about to graduate, and was here to visit his parents before finishing up his last year. As they talked, he eventually asked her if she had ever been to the Jamaica Plains Arboretum.

Maria shrugged. "I don't even know what that is," she admitted.

"Oh, it's fantastic," Matt responded, clearly passionate about all things botanical and not afraid to show it. "There are so many trees and flowers of all shapes and sizes. I'm sure you'd love it."

"You really think so?" she asked.

"Definitely. Right up your alley. You said you go to school near here right? Why don't I pick you up after you get out, and we'll make an afternoon out of it?"

"I . . . guess that would be alright," Maria said. She had only just met him, but he seemed an okay sort, even though she knew next to nothing about him. He made her feel comfortable and he was easy to talk to.

A few hours later, she waited for Matt after school, to carry out their plans as he suggested. But there was so much traffic, so many people moving around that she was afraid he would not be able to find her among the crowd.

Then she found a pair of hands over her eyes, and a familiar voice saying, "Guess who?" Delighted, Maria turned around to see him, smiling and laughing. She was gleeful that he managed to find her. She saw her friend Angie, some distance away, who seemed to notice that she was with a handsome boy. Without saying a word, she gave Maria a nod and a look of approval, and went off her own way.

He took her hand, saying, "Are you ready for this?" His eyes were radiant with joy, far more excited than most others to go and look at plants.

"As ready as I will ever be!" Maria said, just as shamelessly excited as he was.

The time Maria spent at the Arboretum certainly impressed her. Everything from the wrought iron gate flanked by two majestic trees at the entrance to the way the soft grass felt on her bare feet had her captivated. Matt took her on a tour of the whole place, and they walked for many hours. He clearly had been here many times, and was gauging her reaction to everything they came across, whether it was a massive birch tree or a tiny patch of clover.

They rested many times, but still Maria wanted to see more, the magic of this place had her terminally charmed. She felt as though she was in a whole new time and place, surrounded by so much serene green life. Matt said it was refreshing to meet someone else who appreciated simple beauty, and asked her if she wanted to see more. Maria could not agree fast enough. He told her to meet him again at the pond they met at, and they would have their second date.

However, this budding fairy tale romance had a decidedly abrupt life. When Maria went to find him the next day before school, he was nowhere to be found. She waited until she was almost late for school, then sadly left, lamenting that she would not have the chance to see him again, as this was the last day she would cross by this pond, and they still had not exchanged phone numbers. This was the last day of her summer school; there was no reason for her to come out to Jamaica Plains anymore, and certainly her parents would not approve of her going so far for nothing.

When she met up with her friend Angie at school, she immediately picked up on Maria's distress. When she asked what was wrong, Maria explained to her about Matt and their lovely date the day before, and how she could not meet with him that morning. Angie mentioned that she had seen Matt by the boathouse, on the other end of the pond where Maria had been, looking like he was waiting for someone.

That must have been him, she thought, and immediately started to remember him saying the word "boathouse," but she did not think to ask about it or where it was. She had misunderstood him, and would probably never get the chance to see him again. Angie did her best to cheer her up, inviting her to go with Angie and a few of their other friends to go back to the Arboretum that afternoon. Maria agreed, hoping that a return to that beautiful place would help her through her sadness.

The more she thought of it, the more it felt like fate that they were never to cross paths again. She started to wonder what fate had in store for her, as she got into Angie's boyfriends car, and she sat down in the front seat next to the driver.

Next to Marko.

♓♈♓♈♓♈♓♈♓♈♓♈

Not long after the visit to the colossus site, Marko and Maria's honeymoon ended, and they moved to the mainland of Greece. They had a home in Halandry, which was a suburb of Athens. They would spend the workweek there, while Marko started job hunting while working a few days a week as a lounge singer, and on the weekends they traveled to the island of Salamis, where Marko's family lived.

The weekdays were harder for Maria during those first few months. Athens was a busy place, and there would always be something to do, but for her it could be rather lonely. She spent much of her time alone at home, just waiting for Marko to come back. When he did return, it was often too late in the day and he would be too tired to go out and do something.

Still, the people she met everyday were kind enough. The people she got to know everyday, the people in shops and all the places she went day to day, were friendly, warm, and helpful. They made Maria feel like a real part of the community, even though she had only being living there for a short while.

She was quite entertained by the locals as well, their customs and little ways of doing things always made her smile. It was so different from what she was used to. Over time she was able to learn the language just by imitating phrases and sayings she heard in conversations. Whenever she was down, perhaps feeling under the weather, folks used to say she had the look of the "evil eye," and offered to remove it. They would then chant a little prayer, making the sign of the cross as they did, and cough a little bit as they expelled the "evil" of the curse. Maria did not think that it really did anything, though at times she wondered. Regardless, it did make her feel accepted and welcomed, if not just a little bit better.

But the weekends were worth the wait. They would get on the boat and after a short and lovely trip, they would be with Marko's family at their place in Salamis. There, Maria spent time getting to know her new family. She and Ioanna, her mother-in-law, spent plenty of time together during these times, growing on each other in a fortunate fashion. Communication was not easy, as Ioanna did not know English and Maria was just learning

Greek. But through half-sentences and hand signs they made themselves understood.

However, it was Gabriel, Marko's father, that really made the place in Salamis feel like home to Maria. A strong, clean-shaven businessman, always dressed in a vested suit, he was stern of demeanor, but his edges were softened by the kindness of a true family man. All the good things that happened to Maria recently she could attribute directly or indirectly to Gabriel. They had a great relationship now, but she was not so lucky when they first met.

When Marko first brought Maria to meet his family, he spent hours preparing her for the meeting. He instructed her on all kinds of etiquette, what to say, how to say it, when to speak and act, and what would be expected of her. When she finally met Gabriel, her heart raced and her mind buzzed. Stage fright of sorts came over her, for just a moment; what if she did the wrong thing, or said something out of turn?

Steeling herself as he approached, he offered his hand and she kissed the back of it, a simple and classic sign of respect. He quietly approved of her gesture, inviting her to sit with the family. She let her breath go; the first step had been taken.

As it turned out, Gabriel knew quite a bit of English. Maria took this to heart, as she knew English better than Greek. She wanted to be able to converse with him, this impressive man she had come to know. However, he was usually serious and standoffish around her, as though he had some unknown disdain for her.

One fateful Sunday, Marko was to play in an exhibition soccer game. His whole family was there, and she would be sitting with them.

Maria quite liked sports, and was a bit of an athlete herself. She loved competition and was easily excited by the nature of most sports. She initially tried to keep her enthusiasm under control, but she quickly lost her inhibitions about such worries. She was whooping and hollering with the whole crowd in no time, fully lost in the heat of the game. At one point, she shouted very loudly, and heard another voice nearby join in, and she turned to see Gabriel hollering alongside her. He shot her a big smile, his joy quite apparent. After the game, Gabriel approached her. "So energetic! You must really like sports."

"I do, they're very exciting," Maria said. "I didn't know you were a fan, either."

Gabriel laughed. "Sometimes, sometimes. Your enthusiasm is contagious, my girl." He paused, thoughtful for a moment. "Do you want to marry Marko?"

Maria stopped cold, taken aback by his words. "Shouldn't Marko ask me first?"

Gabriel smirked. "If he was not serious about you, he never would have brought you to meet me." He grew serious for a moment. "I would be honored if you would join our family."

Maria lost her ability to speak for a moment. *Gabriel* would be honored if *she* would join his family! Her mouth dry and heart throbbing, she explained that she would need time to tell her parents. Gabriel agreed, and told her that he wanted to speak to them as well.

That night, Marko officially proposed to her, and she accepted. There was no other way things could be.

Maria then took up the daunting task of telling her parents she was going to be married at seventeen years old in just a few months. Her mother's reaction was typical, yelling and screaming and threatening her with life in a convent. Maria could hardly blame her, the idea had been so sudden and shocking to her at first. She had a plan for her life before, and now she was changing everything. What happened to her becoming a journalist with her best friend Sandra, like they said they would do back when they were with their high school's newsletter? What about becoming a professional businesswoman? She felt that could wait, life was happening. She did not back down, sticking to her decision and showing she was committed to this path. In time, they calmed down enough that she could talk to them seriously. Still, they were unsure that she was ready. Maria told them that Gabriel wanted to talk to them, and he might be able to assuage their fears. Tentatively, they agreed.

When Gabriel came to speak with her parents, they welcomed him politely but sternly. It was clear that he was going to have to impress them incredibly to sway them at all.

Gabriel seemed to understand that, and told them as much right away. He sympathized with their fears and worries, and knew how important Maria must be to them. He promised that they would not have to worry about her well being, he would personally see that she was cared for, and would be loved as one of their own. He explained that there was a place for them to spend time in Salamis before the wedding and see where their daughter was going to make her home. He ended by expressing how proud they must be of Maria, and asked again for their consent.

So heartfelt and sincere was Gabriel's speech that Maria's mother was in tears. Her parents agreed, still somewhat reluctant. Afterward, Gabriel brought out some fantastic wine, and they all toasted to a future they all would share together. Soon everyone was happy and celebrating; their future was going to be a happy one. Maria caught Gabriel's glance, and he winked. She was going to be in good hands.

Gabriel took to young Maria very well after that, making her a part of the family almost instantly, from the moment she arrived back in Greece for the wedding. Gabriel tried to include her in everything they did after that, always taking the time to make sure she was happy, watching out for her wellbeing and helping her whenever he could. Gabriel was another kind of blessing to Maria, a second father.

On those days in Salamis, the whole family would often go out to do various activities. Maria's favorite had to be going to the various beaches. The glorious sandy beaches of Greece never seemed to be too crowded but neither were they lonely and empty. The water, sunshine, and all of the people were an exquisite experience, made even better when spending it with the excellent family she had managed to make herself a part of.

Her mother-in-law taught her a great trick for those long days at the beach. They would mix up some bread and feta cheese with a little water, and roll it into a ball. They placed the mixture into a large basin, and stretch netting across the top, cutting a small slit in the center. Leaving it deep in the water, they simply enjoyed the rest of the day, and they would come back when they were ready to leave and retrieve the basin. Every time they would have caught several fish, perfect for taking home to eat that night.

Some evenings they went out to a local dinner and dance club. There was always a live band making the night come alive with music, people enjoying themselves at tables and on the dance floor. After a delicious meal, Maria joined the other dancers, sometimes alone, sometimes with Marko, and even on a few occasions with Gabriel and even Ioanna. Gabriel made her smile, made her laugh, and above all made her feel safe. She was more a part of the family than she ever could have been thanks to her father in law.

It was a shame, then, that Marko did not get along very well with his own father. Their argument was an absolutely classic tale; Gabriel desired for his son to settle down and be a respectable business man, but Marko had his heart set on making a living being a musician. The two of them clashed on many, frequent occasions, but underneath it all, Maria could see that Gabriel only wanted the best for the two of them. Whenever Marko fought him on this matter, he would always tell him, "You have a family of your own now, you need to provide for them!"

Maria looked at her life one of these weekends, really thinking about her place in the world. After much deliberation, she considered herself lucky. She lived in one of the most beautiful places in the world, full of culture and history. She had found someone she loved and would spend her life with. She was safe, financially secure, and healthy, emotionally and physically. Most of all, she had not one but two families, both of which gave her all the support she would ever need.

The only thing that could make the time more beautiful was a child to call her own.

♓♑♓♑♓♑♓♑♓♑

The April following Maria and Marko's marriage, Maria learned that she was with child. The world seemed colored with a brighter brush that day. The news was spread quickly among friends and family, and with every congratulations or blessing sent her way, the brightness inside her grew brighter.

But no matter how much her light grew, nothing could compare to the radiance on Gabriel's beaming face the first time he saw her after hearing the wonderful news. He hugged her and kissed her cheeks, expressing his barely contained happiness with a variety of affections. She knew just how he was feeling, their family was going to be one little person bigger, and one person happier.

That night, she heard Marko and Gabriel arguing again, somewhat louder than usual. Marko seemed to be trying to argue that he would be fine going into a career in music, but Gabriel was more firm than ever about him settling down to raise his family in a reliable way. Maria heard it all from her bed, and she clutched the sheets tight to herself, considering if her own child would fight like that with its father in the coming years. Maybe that was all a part of family life, she told herself, taking the good with the bad. Satisfied with the answer, she settled back in to sleep, even as Marko and Gabriel argued on.

She and Marko spent much of the coming months in Athens, where they found a good and respectable doctor to help care for Maria during her pregnancy. Together with Marko, she traversed markets and stores looking for all the things that a baby would need when it was born. Their small apartment was only a one bedroom, so one of the things they would have to look for in the near future was another home with a place of the baby to grow and play. But there would be time for that later. For now they looked at cradles and strollers, bottles and bibs, diapers and blankets, toys and mobiles, all in a dizzying whirl of a few months.

The next few months were fraught with worry, excitement, and copious amounts of planning. As the delivery date grew nearer, Maria began to obsess over all kinds of details for the baby, everything from the size of the crib to the temperature in the house at night, which could get a little chilly. Marko often became exasperated, and constantly told her to calm down, But that did not deter her one bit. If she could manage to do something right for her child, she would make absolutely sure that it was done.

One thing Maria made sure to improve during this time was her cooking. She had always wanted to hone her cooking skills, and this was the perfect time to start. She already fancied herself a decent cook, but there was always room for improvement. She tested out new recipes, everything from local dishes to interesting ones from cookbooks were added to her repertoire. All the while she made changes to old ones, finding new techniques and ideas to make her old favorites special again. She considered herself lucky having experienced culinary delights from Portugal, Venezuela, the United States, and Greece in her short life. She adored all the different spices, textures, and would try any food before deciding if it was something to consider adding to her ever expanding cookbook.

Eventually, Gabriel found out that Maria was expanding her cooking abilities, and came by to try some of her work. Maria toiled over a splendid meal to impress her father in law, putting all of her new skills to the test. The meal was served to the whole family, and not a single sour look or hesitant bite was made.

Gabriel seemed rather impressed. After the meal, he told her, "You're very good, Maria. I should give you a few recipes for you to try out."

"Baba, you can cook?" Maria asked, delighted.

"Absolutely! You think I'm just another pretty face?" He laughed heartily. "I'll look through some recipes, and I'll show you some of my favorites."

Gabriel did exactly as he said, coming to share a new recipe time after time with Maria to add to her growing cookbook. He was quite creative in the kitchen, but at the same time practical and practiced. Maria relished those cooking lessons, as both a means to expand on her new hobby, and a way to bond with Gabriel.

He showed her how to make so many different things, from roast lamb with lemon sauce, to the very unusual squid stew. But her favorite had to be his perfect fasolada, a delicious Cannelli bean stew. The day he showed her, he brought over all the ingredients, and explained it to her.

"You must make sure it's prepared separately, the beans and the vegetables," he said sternly, after explaining the rest of the recipe. "The beans must be nice and tender before they're added to the other vegetables, or it won't come out right." He waved his hands toward the ingredients. "You try, all on your own. See if you can impress me!"

Maria accepted his challenge with gusto. She went right to work, giving her all to the task, and trying to follow his instructions exactly. This is how most of her lessons with Gabriel went, he would explain every step, every detail of a recipe, and then let her try it out herself, letting her figure it out and make mistakes along the way. From lesson to lesson, she got some of it right and did a few things wrong, but she got more right and less wrong each time.

Finally she was ready to share her creation with the rest of the family. She was worried that she did not let the beans get tender enough, she felt she added the vegetables too soon. But once Gabriel had tried it, her fears were dispelled by his big grin as he got another spoonful.

Maria continued to enjoy cooking for the whole time she was pregnant. Even after Gabriel had exhausted his recipe list, she continued to search out new and interesting techniques and dishes.

One night late in December, she and Marko had over a couple they were friends with, Felix and Rosa, and she made an excellent chicken fricassee—one of Ioanna's recipes—with celery stalks and a special sauce she had been experimenting with, trying to perfect. She was certain she made it just right that time, judging by the gleeful reactions of her company.

It was a fine dinner besides. The conversation was witty and enjoyable, the atmosphere was pleasant and relaxed, everything seemed to be going just right. Everyone had just finished eating and they decided it would be a great idea to have a game of cards. While Marko went and looked for the cards, Maria took some of the dirty dishes into the kitchen.

That was when Maria felt something trickle down her leg. Her first reaction was that she spilled something on herself. She started to put the dishes in the sink when she heard liquid splash all over the floor. She realized suddenly that her water just broke. Ready or not, the baby was coming.

At first she was torn: she could not decide whether she was happy, or if she was frightened. The baby was finally ready! All of what that meant washed over her a few seconds, which seemed like minutes to poor Maria. In short order however, she decided panic was the best option.

"Marko!" she shouted, coming back to the other room. "The baby is coming!"

Marko looked shocked at first, then shook his head. "The only way you could have ruined this evening Maria . . . it's a happy way, but the only way . . ."

Felix offered to drive them to the hospital in his car, which Maria agreed to readily. She did not want to have to sit around waiting for a taxi while the baby was trying to get out. They all got into his car, and sped off toward the hospital.

Maria soon regretted her decision to forgo a taxi. Felix's car was a firebird, a very low to the ground vehicle that had poor suspension. Every dip and bump in the road was felt keenly throughout the car, making Maria cringe and wince every time they turned. She was almost positive that the car fishtailed more than a few times on the turns.

She had been in no pain when they had got to in the car, but by the time they arrived at the hospital, she was starting to get quite uncomfortable. Whether that was due to the crazy ride or just a natural progression for childbirth, she was not sure.

Getting Maria out of the vehicle also proved to be a challenge. Being so low to the ground and having a belly the size of a watermelon on her lap, along with the discomfort she was starting to feel quite acutely, it was nearly impossible for her to do by herself. In the end, both Marko and Felix had to help her out of the car, both taking one of her hands and lifting her out.

Once they were in the building, their admitting nurse gave Marko a stack of paperwork and told Maria to sit in a wheelchair and come along with her. She barely had time to tell him goodbye, and he barely looked up from the papers to wave to her as she was hurried out of the room. Little did she know, that was the last time she would see him for over twenty hours.

The nurse brought her to the labor and delivery area of the hospital, deep down in the hospital. Maria could swear she was it was in the basement by how far down she felt she was. The windows in her room were tiny and above her eye level, making the room feel very dark and secluded. The colors that were chosen for what should have been a happy place were all so dreary. Maroon walls with cream trim and black doors and windows gave her the distinct impression of some sort of high class mortuary, not a delivery room.

She was left alone in that little room for quite a while. Her labor pains were beginning to grow more intense, and fear began to mount where anticipation had been. Was it supposed to hurt this bad? She felt as though something was seriously wrong. She called out for help, but no one came. It then occurred to her: in just a couple hours it would be Christmas Eve! Many of the staff were probably out on vacation, was she actually all alone here now?

No, wait. She strained her ears to hear beyond the room, down the hall. She could barely make out the sounds of singing, a Christmas carol she could not quite place. There were other people here!

The pain was unbearable, and it came in waves. It was very strong at times, so much that she thought her baby would just break right through her belly. Then it would subside and let her breathe again. Every time the pain started its upward course she would give out a muffled scream. Was this how it was supposed to be? Was she supposed to lay down, on her back or her side? Was she supposed to sit up or walk around? No one had told her what to expect, much less what she should do, and the thought that she was alone for this made her mad with fright.

She shouted much louder, and moments later a crusty old nurse came in, a scowl on her face. "You aren't the only one having a baby, you know! Keep quiet, it's not that bad!"

Before Maria could tell her otherwise, she stormed out. Distraught, she laid back down, trying to deal with the now quite serious pains. She heard moments later the muffled sounds of an argument just outside the door, and another nurse came into her room, of a somewhat more sympathetic disposition.

"What's the matter?" she asked. Maria told here that she felt something was wrong, and that she hurt very badly. She bombarded the nurse with the questions she had, desperate to get this right. The nurse calmly answered everything she asked, checked on her and the baby by feeling around her belly, and said, "Well, the baby is breached. We'll have to do something about that."

Maria's fear spiked for a moment, as she wondered what they were going to do to her, but all it turned out to be was she needed to rub her belly clockwise, firmly, as so to help the baby start slowly turning around and face downward, ready to come out the right way. That, coupled with the nurse talking her through how to breathe through the pain, helped make the pain a little more tolerable. The nurse had to leave her after a short time, but at least she had helped.

After rubbing her stomach for what seemed like hours, she finally felt the baby flip around inside her, and immediately the horrible pain diminished to a much more bearable level. The contractions were still happening, and they were still quite painful, but not nearly as bad as it was before.

After some time, Maria was committed to the idea that it was going to hurt. Every labor pain was like a knife, but she steeled herself each time. Compared to how it was when the baby was breached, it was like running a race instead of being dragged along by a car. Eventually she reached the point where she did not even flinch at the contractions.

Many hours of labor passed, and though she knew there must have been a doctor in the room she was not aware of anyone else. For Maria, it was just her and the baby now. With every breath she just focused on the image that she had in her mind of her baby slowly and steadily moving out of her body. When it was all over and the baby was out, the relief was so overwhelming that she must have passed out.

Maria awoke hours later, elsewhere in the hospital. Marko was nowhere to be found. She started calling out for someone, anyone, to come to her. Eventually the nurses learned she was awake, and they came into her room. She had lots of questions and wanted to ask them all at once. The nurses started answering her questions and giving her the information she desired. Her baby was a boy, he was perfectly fine, and she had experienced some unexpected hemorrhaging and required a transfusion. It was under control now, but she had been out for a few hours, and still needed to rest. She would need to stay for a five to six more days.

Doing as she was told, she managed to doze off for a few hours at a time while a parade of nursing staff came by with questions and instructions. They tried to tell her so many things: how to bathe the baby, how to breastfeed, and many other suggestions and bits of advice were given. Maria nodded and listened, and was grateful, but she already knew it all. She had been studying hard on how to take care of her little one, she knew what needed to be done.

Even so, her heart filled with apprehension for the future. There was so much that could go wrong, things she never even considered before she held a tiny life in her arms. She knew what to do, of course. All the knowledge was fresh in her mind. But there was a nagging doubt that something could go wrong. When she bathed him, would the water be too hot? Or too cold? Would she drop him by accident? What else might go wrong?

She decided in the end that she would just have to do the best she could. There was only so much you could prepare for; some things just had to be done. Experience would be the best teacher, nothing in a book could compare to the knowledge she would get just from trying.

It was decided long ago that if the baby was a boy, by an old Greek tradition he would be named after Marko's father, Gabriel. Five days later, She and Marko brought little Gabriel home for the first time.

It seemed that the good times were about to get better, as a few months after Little Gabriel was born, Marko's father arrived during the week at their place in Halandry with some good news. He wanted to be closer to the newest member of the family, so he had purchased a pair of condominiums in a new development at the edge of the city. One of them, the smaller of the two, was for him, his wife and their son. The one attached to it, much larger for a growing family, was for Maria, Marko, and their baby. Maria was overcome with gratitude, Gabriel had given them so much already, this latest gesture was so much more than she ever could have wanted.

They went out to look at the new buildings later that day, and Maria was even more impressed. The building was amazing; two smaller homes joined together, just like their family was now. There was a beautiful terrace, big enough for a dining set so they could eat outside, basking in the magnificent view of the city while they supped. They took down the interior divider, allowing free access between the two houses. Doing so turned two homes into one big home for them all. The terrace wrapped around to the side of the building all the way across the back, the perfect place for a growing child to play.

It was all so perfect to Maria. There was nothing more she could have asked for in a home. Between her new home and her newborn son, she believed this joy would last forever.

Maria and Gabriel weeks after born

PART II

Hope, Retreating

Not long after Gabriel was born, Maria and Marko found themselves traveling back and forth between their homes in Athens and America. It seemed as though the little family was stuck between two worlds, not quite satisfied with either. Every six months or so, there would be something that came up, an obligation or an opportunity that inspired them to move again. The constant traveling was starting to tire Maria out, and it was a lot of work for poor Little Gabriel to have to keep up with. She expressed her feelings to Marko, telling him that they needed to settle down sooner or later, for the good of their son.

Marko seemed to understand the situation, but he never made a commitment to either home. There was plenty of opportunity in America, to be sure. They were much more likely to find success on their own in America. But Marko had too many ties and obligations back in Greece to make a permanent move to the States. At times he would entertain the idea, and they would look at houses in either country. Sometimes they would even discuss buying a plot of land to build their own place, but nothing ever came of it. There was always some "great opportunity" for Marko's musical career somewhere, or there was an "amazing job offer" from someone he knew. So for about two years, they crossed the ocean many times, bouncing between two countries.

However, it was in the States where they got the call that changed everything. They were at their little apartment in Jamaica Plains, and Maria was watching Little Gabriel as he played with his blocks. The phone rang in the other room, and Marko picked up the phone. Maria expected him to yell, he often yelled at the phone nowadays. But the customary shout never came.

Intrigued, Maria got up to check on him, leaving little Gabriel to his toys. When she got to the kitchen, she just saw Marko, sitting at the table, the phone in his hand emitting a dial tone. He looked very cross, but in a very different way than Maria was used to.

"Is something the matter?" she asked.

Marko just looked at her, his eyes dull and sullen.

"Who was on the phone?" Maria asked, growing concerned.

"It was my mother," Marko finally answered. All life had left his voice.

"Is she okay?" Maria asked.

"My father just died."

Maria's breath simply left her. So long did she wait to breathe again that she counted five heartbeats. The quiet in the room as they both sat struck with silence was punctuated only with little Gabriel's gleeful chirps from the next room. Somehow she managed to make it to a chair before she slumped to the floor. This news was so shocking, so unexpected, that she simply was not prepared to deal with the information. Even though she had so many questions, all of her emotions careened against themselves, rendering her speechless. She felt tears rolling unabated down her cheeks, but did not feel herself sobbing.

"What are we going to do now, Marko?" she asked in a broken voice minutes later.

"We have to go back again," he said, "at least for the funeral, and the reading of the will."

She nodded, registering his words but not fully understanding. Still, she could not comprehend how awful this news was, and Marko seemed to be taking it very well. He must have been raging inside though, and just thinking of what he must be feeling pushed her over the edge into sobbing. Marko held her while she cried, gently and tenderly for the first time in quite a while, while her heart mourned enough for both of them.

They packed and were ready to leave within a few hours. They found out later in the week that the funeral was going to happen quite soon, in two days in fact. There was no embalming, so the funeral needed to happen very soon after death. Gabriel Senior's decline was more apparent than Maria and Marko were aware, it seemed. His condition had been noticeably declining ever since their last trip back to America, coming to a sad crescendo in the past few weeks. Maria had grown fond of thinking that Gabriel Senior would be around for a long time, spending days with his grandson, loving him and protecting him. To think they had lost him so soon was a terrible thing. The worst of it was that Little Gabriel would never get to know his grandfather. There was so much that Gabriel could have taught him, and so much they could have learned together. All of that was gone, never to be realized.

During the following days, Maria noticed a subtle change in Marko. He seemed to be quieter, as though he was considering something that weighed heavily on his mind. As much as she was concerned for him, Maria decided against talking to him about what bothered him. He was already under enough emotional stress; there was no telling what would push him over the edge. She tried to be as supportive and caring as possible, but left him to his thoughts when she noticed him brooding on his unknown troubles.

The only way they would be able to get there on time was to take an over eight hour flight directly to Greece. It would be exhausting, especially for the baby, but they had no other choice. On the flight, Maria worried that little Gabriel would not take to the long flight very well, but the young child seemed to be rather calm about the whole ordeal. Maria got the idea that her son was aware that something was not right, and kept quiet to try and figure out what was going on. Once or twice, he started crying, but all Maria had to do was hold him and shush him gently, and he was quiet again, put at ease by his mother's touch and voice. Soon, all the activity of late got to him and he was fast asleep.

They arrived very late in the morning to Greece. By the time they got there, got on a taxi to get to Piraeus, and took the ferry to Salamis, the funeral procession was already scheduled to begin.

They got on yet another taxi and raced around town to find the procession. They almost collided with the line when they found it, but after the confusion had passed they were allowed to join the procession to the funeral directly behind the hearse. From their car Maria could see Gabriel's coffin in the back. The pit of her stomach seemed to grow deeper as it all became so much more real. Up until now it had been so far away, and now the reality of Gabriel's death was literally right in front of her, and she found herself unable to express what she was feeling.

The funeral was unlike anything Maria had been to before. The casket was left open, and people stood in a long line to pay their respects individually. When it was her and Marko's turn, she went numb, at least at first. What was she supposed to do, what was she supposed to say? There was nothing where all emotion should be, so drained and sick this all made her feel.

Marko touched her arm. "Is there anything you want to say to him, Maria?"

His touch, his voice, put it all together for her. The finality of it, the sorrow and pain, the feeling of loss all overwhelmed her at once. She could never speak to him again. She would never see him when she came back to Salamis again. Tears started rolling down her cheeks, and her throat choked up as she looked to Marko. "Would it be alright if I . . . if I kissed him goodbye?"

Marko nodded, and Maria stepped up to the casket, hesitantly at first, her feet and legs denying the orders of her mind. Gabriel's head rested on a small pillow. She leaned over and kissed him on the forehead, wishing him a final goodbye. Somehow, just then, she felt . . . serenity, a sense of calm that pervaded her slowly but utterly. She had made her peace, and given a final gesture of her love; doing so made her much more at ease. All at once, she heard the mourners begin to cry and lament, as though bidden to do so by her actions. It seemed so unreal, that moment.

It occurred to Maria that she had no idea how Gabriel had died. She asked Ioanna in private later how he had died, but she would only say that it must have been his time to meet with God. Maria felt comfortable leaving it at that. His death had been rather mysterious; he seemed to fall ill for no reason, or perhaps a reason he did not share with anyone. It was just assumed it was his time to go.

The ride home was a complete blur. Jetlag was catching up with them. So much had happened in such a short space of time, and without enough rest to help her keep up with it all. When they got back to the family house, she wearily asked if she could lie down. Ioanna told her it was fine, and said she could use the bed in her room.

When she arrived at the bed, it took all of her will to keep from simply collapsing onto it. The moment she made herself comfortable, she was asleep. She dreamed turbulently for some time, a jumble of images and thoughts that blended together in uncomfortable ways. So tired was Maria that it all just washed over her in a dizzying sea of confusion.

She was woken a short time later when she felt someone sit down at the edge of the bed.

"Marko? Is that you?" she asked deliriously. Her eyes would not work for her, even though they would open they could not focus.

"No, Maria," the person said. "It's me."

Maria forced her eyes to try and work, blinking several times. She tried to lift herself up but had no strength yet.

"It's okay, I am right here," he said, shifting closer to her position.

"But what are you doing here?"

"I came to say goodbye," he said, and Maria could hear the smile in his voice. "I owe you something still." He leaned in gave her a great big hug. He kissed her cheek, his rough stubbly beard scratching her face. "One for me, and one for you, eh?"

Maria was able to bring her arms around to hug him. She knew once she let go, it was for good. For a long time, she just laid there, hanging on to him and praying that it did not end, that it could go on for just a minute longer.

Eventually, he pulled away, holding her at arms length, smiling calmly and warmly. For a second, Maria was able to focus her eyes, and the first thing she saw was Gabriel before he faded away.

"NO!" Her strength came back with fear, and she bolted upright in bed. Tears streamed down her face, and she reached out to where he had been.

Ioanna and Marko rushed into the room then. "Maria! What happened? What's the matter?" Ioanna asked.

Maria started to explain what had happened, in a shaky, tearful voice. She told them everything, but started to doubt her own words. The more she spoke of it, the more it started to sound foolish, and started to think it was all some sort of dream.

Ioanna just sat and listened while she talked, and after a while seemed to be intent on a spot on her face. When Maria was finished, Ioanna brought her had up to Maria's face, touching her cheek. Maria flinched, the spot felt scratched and hot.

"Is that where he kissed you?" Ioanna asked softly.

Maria nodded, brushing her cheek again, remembering his rough, salt and pepper beard.

Ioanna smiled. "He really liked you, Maria. He must have wanted to give you one last goodbye."

Maria nodded, keeping her hand on her cheek. She rested herself back again, unsure of what really happened but certain that she was going to sleep easier.

"Mama Sou"

The next few days they took rather slow. Unwilling to jump back on a plane just yet, with so many things to attend to, they were in no rush to get home. There was simply a void now where Gabriel used to be, and it seemed to draw in time like a vortex. Everything just seemed to drag on, even easy tasks were arduous in the face of Gabriel's absence. He meant so much to everyone, and without him around there was a distinct lack of energy.

Maria spent most of her time with Ioanna and Little Gabriel, trying to make herself available for Ioanna to just spend time with when she did not have to be anywhere. Maria had been rather close to her to begin with, but now she felt they needed to stick together more than ever now; one of the most wonderful men in both their lives was gone forever.

They eventually decided to stay in Greece for an extended period. It was clear their presence was needed here now more than back in America. They had nothing to hurry back to, at least nothing that warranted the expense of a plane ticket, and they had very little desire to leave the family in such a sorry state.

Marko asked one day about the reading of the will, bringing up the issue of inheritance. Maria had never considered it, but Gabriel had been quite a wealthy man, and his wealth would have to go somewhere. She supposed that Ioanna would get it for the most part, but that did not mean that Marko was out in the cold.

A few days later the reading of the will took place. The whole family was present for it, but Maria excused herself from the event. When Ioanna asked her why she did not want to come, she admitted that as much as she was a part of the family, she did not feel she belonged at such a private event.

But personally, she did not feel that she could be around people talking about Gabriel back when he was alive and he knew he was going to die. That would just be too much for her to handle.

Besides, she felt she had already been the recipient of his "last words," and his kiss goodbye was all she could have ever asked from him. In all her life she never met anyone like him, with a beautiful heart, impeccable character, and shining with dignity. He impressed upon her like no other; he was absolutely unforgettable. To ask for more was unacceptable.

The family was gone for a few hours, leaving Maria alone at the family house. Bored and restless, she decided she would do some cooking, preparing a meal for the rest when they got back. She went to the kitchen, to see what she could find to make.

The moment she started looking, however, she realized that these were all things Gabriel had used to make food for his family. At some point he had used all these things, the saucepan, the ladle, the tongs, the strainer, all of them he had touched, had made food with them. He deemed them good enough to use, good enough for his family.

Maria backed out of the kitchen quietly, disheartened and somehow ashamed. She felt as though she was intruding, she did not deserve to make food where he had worked his cooking magic. It was not her place, it was almost sacred now. It was because of him she was as skilled as she was at cooking, and she was about to use his kitchen without permission. She went back out into the sitting room, to wait patiently in the shadow of a great man.

Soon, the rest of the family was back. Marko seemed to be in a foul mood, everyone else was simply dour. Maria found out later that it was much as she had figured; Ioanna inherited most of Gabriel's belongings. Marko, his younger brother Stavros, and his older sister Lysandra, or Lysa as her family called her, all inherited money as well, but it was through a trust fund that was held by Ioanna.

"That's not so bad," Maria said to Marko.

"He didn't trust me," Marko said. "He must have thought I'd be so irresponsible."

"He did," Ioanna said. Marko turned to her, anger in his face. "Marko, you have never had a real job your whole life!"

"Only because I wanted to be a singer!" Marko raged. "Just because I have aspirations of being more than just another lowly worker, he thought I would be irresponsible!"

"You never proved him wrong, Marko," Ioanna told him. "You never got the chance to show him that you can do it, that you can do honest hard work."

"Of course I can! Anyone can do it!" Marko argued.

"Well then, if it's so easy, why don't you go and get a job to support your family?" Ioanna retorted. "You need to show me now that you can do this. If you can hold a normal job for a month, I will give you your whole trust fund. You can do whatever you want for a career, no questions asked."

"Ha! You have a deal!" Marko said.

The next day, arrangements were made for Marko to interview at a shoe factory in a few days. He left early the day of the interview in high spirits, proclaiming to Maria that they would be rich at the end of the month.

Over breakfast, Maria asked Ioanna what kind of work he would be doing.

"Oh, it's quite easy," Ioanna told her. "It's just putting pieces together. The pay is nice, and the hours will keep him occupied. I think this will be quite good for him, he may learn a little bit of respect from this." As an afterthought, she added, "He will even still have the weekends to work on his music. How could it go wrong?"

Maria nodded, understanding full well that Marko could be just a little disrespectful of others. "Do you think that he will be able to get the job?"

"Definitely," Ioanna said. "It's a simple job, and the owner is a friend of the family. Trust me, he will do fine there."

A couple of hours later, Marko stormed back in to the family house. His face was red and furious, simmering with rage.

"You're home early . . . did it really go poorly?" Maria asked.

"No," Marko said, "of course it didn't; a fool could do that job."

"Then what happened?" she asked, curious.

"I wouldn't be caught dead working there," Marko said. "Everyone there is an idiot! To think that my mother thought this would be a good job for me!"

"But Marko . . ."

"I refuse to work for a bunch of inferior intellects!" Marko proclaimed. "I'll find something else to do, but I just will not work there!"

Maria sighed. "Whatever you say." She had not thought he would be so obstinate about what he would do for work. She was not terribly disappointed about him losing the deal with Ioanna, not for her sake but for his. She believed that going through with it and keeping his word would have boosted his self confidence, but the fact that Marko was willfully throwing away an easy opportunity because of pride made the pit of her stomach sink in despair.

Over the next few days, it seemed like Marko was going to keep his word. He went out every day to find work, determined to make the deal with his mother work. But everyday he came home with nothing to show.

Maria started to think that perhaps this was a good thing. After so many failed attempts, eventually Marko would realize that the job at the factory was perfectly fine for now, and he was just being picky. Maybe they would even be able to settle down for once; that thought alone was comforting.

As time went on, the opposite seemed to happen. Marko just seemed to give up on finding real work, and settled for the meager sum he would get from the trust fund. He spent less time at home as well, going out at night and often not returning until the next morning. Other times he would simply leave without notice, and did not return for days at a time.

Maria knew where he was, though. That was never a mystery. The evidence was in the smell that hung like a cloud around him, the odor of drinks and partying.

She brushed it off every time, figuring that this was just a phase of married life that she would somehow need to push through to get past to something else, something a little more stable.

Outside of Marko's troubles, her life was starting to look up again. She spent more time with Ioanna and Lysa, and plenty of time with Gabriel. Her little son seemed to be growing up so fast, getting bigger and smarter by the day. He was her joy in these dark times: his smile could turn around a bad day faster than anything else.

Her health was good as well, aside from one or two times she needed to go see her doctor. They were always just minor feminine problems, of course, and the doctor always had an easy way to fix them. Antibiotics, she found, were useful things, they seemed to do the trick every time. She didn't think she would need them so often, especially this young. Taking care of herself and her health was very important, especially now that she had little Gabriel to care for.

Once, while she was getting dressed, she overheard Marko and the doctor arguing outside the exam room. The doctor seemed to be accusing Marko of something, and said he would tell Maria if he found out one more time.

After they left, Marko said that he didn't care for the new hospital policies, and told her they would find a different doctor at another hospital.

Maria mentioned one day when Marko was still around and sober that she wanted to go back to America. She missed her parents and her other family, and wanted to see them again. Secretly, she also hoped that Marko would find something for work in America. Even if that kept them on the other side of the ocean for a long time, she did not want to miss a chance to get him grounded again.

He agreed, mentioning that he might have more luck over there. Maria was delighted, glad that he was thinking the same things as she was. Later she found out he had made several plans for his musical career once they got back to America.

Still she held out hope. Things would get better soon. They had to.

PART III

A Most Important Decision

Maria sat quietly with Gabriel as he played at the kitchen table. They had moved back to Jamaica Plains at Marko's whim, which seemed to be the only reason he did anything nowadays. They lived now in a small, one bedroom apartment, which they managed to furnish pleasantly—but sparsely—with the meager amount of funds they had access to. It was a home, humble though it was. He always said it would last until he got his big break, then they would have something bigger.

Maria was beginning to doubt that such an occurrence would ever come about. Every now and again he would get a gig singing, but all they really had to live off of was his trust fund. Maria had hoped he would see reason or succumb to desperation and start looking for a regular job, but he simply refused to. Friends would tell him of job opportunities that he would agree to apply to, only to keep the job for a few weeks. Sometimes he would just leave the house without saying anything, and not return for days. These occasions, unfortunately, happened more and more often, leaving Maria feeling helpless. Uncertainty dominated her future now, like a shadow in a doorway.

Marko was gone again, it had been three days since she saw him last. She was not worried, despite that; she knew where he was. Not exactly where, but as to what he was doing there could be no question.

He thought she did not know what he did, that much was sure. But Maria was not a fool; she learned long ago exactly what he was up to when he left like this. There had been rumors and comments by their friends' wives, often showing a great deal of concern for her with their probing. Marko acted like it was no big deal when he returned, like he had just come home from work, but Maria could smell his indiscretions all over him.

"Mama Sou"

She smelled liquor, like the kind they served in coffee houses, the kind he and his friends liked to frequent—not the Kafeneios that his father used to frequent, fine establishments for gentlemen to play cards, share stories, and drink Turkish coffee. She smelled perfume, on him and his clothes, a scent she did not wear herself, the kind that hookers and tramps liked. He was not away at work; he only wanted to play.

Not that his work was much better. His band was not doing much better, the money he got from gigs was not very much, and gigs were infuriatingly infrequent at best. Most of the work he got was during the summer, at festivals. Winters saw a substantial drop in his business. All he really got for money was his trust fund, barely enough to sustain their tiny family.

Family. That word had a much different meaning now, after the few years she had been with Marko. Four years seemed like many more because of all the travel, bouncing between homes, but it was just four years. He married her, but she understood why. At some point it may have included love, but that was not his reason.

She remembered clearly the day he told her exactly why he married her. They were getting ready for a night out at the theater, and he was inspecting her outfit, making sure everything from her hair down to the brooch she wore pleased him. It was a matter of station; someone like him should be married to someone nice.

And that's all Maria was to him; a nice girl that he could mold to his purpose. His family had been waiting for him to bring home a bride, and he did not disappoint them. She was young, had a fair complexion, a trim figure, a charming smile, and was untouched by other lovers. If he had failed to find a suitable wife, his inheritance would have been at risk. Family was important, but for Marko it was all about appearances. For him, family was an excuse not to try.

His complete disregard for Maria made her sick. He abandoned her at the apartment in Jamaica Plain, leaving her and Gabriel to fend for themselves while he indulged himself. She had no way to drive, was often left with little money in her purse, and was miles from the nearest store. She had to walk those long distances with Gabriel, often needing to make more than one trip so she could get more than one bag of groceries at a time.

She often pitied little Gabriel, who was caught in the middle of this. He loved his daddy, to be sure, but it seemed to Maria that even her little boy could tell that something was not right.

Out of nowhere, she heard keys in the front door. Before Maria could understand what was happening, little Gabriel had jumped out of his chair and was off to the front door, excited to see his dad. Maria got up to follow, but did so quite slowly. She was not so eager to see Marko again, and wanted him to know.

Marko was indeed back, and he was standing in the living room a cocky expression on his face. Little Gabriel was facing him and walking backward as Marko came in closer. Maria tensed, as though he might attack her. Before he left, they had a fight, in which she told him he needed to be more responsible, and he had made it clear that she had no say in the way he lived his life. By the way he carried himself, he seemed confident that his disappearance had in some way shown her that he was right. Being twelve years her senior, he always thought he was right around her. Her defiance was a phase, soon she would see reason and accept that this was how life was.

"Are you ready to be a good girl now, Maria?" Marko said, crossing his arms.

Maria became so very angry at his words. After being gone for days, not even a phone call, he dared to utter such debasing words! How could he have the nerve to insinuate *she* was in the wrong here? How selfish could one man be? Gabriel looked over at her, as though he read her mind, expecting her to be angry. If she did not stand up for herself now, what would she be teaching Gabriel?

"I am always a good girl," she replied sternly. "Are you ready to be a good boy?"

Marko's face contorted in rage, and he made a move like he was going to hit her, but he stopped cold. Maria was not sure what made him stop, until she looked down and saw Gabriel, his little hands grasping his father's legs.

"Daddy, please no fight!" Gabriel cried out.

Maria stood dumbfounded as though Marko had indeed struck her. Those words from her only son shook her deeper than any physical blow could have. Her boy was the bravest person in the world at that moment, braver than she could ever be.

She looked back at Marko, who was trying hard not to be angry with his son. This man was not going to change. Maria knew then and there that she needed to keep her son away from the situations Marko created, and the anger and sadness he was sure to foster in the boy over time. There was so much lacking between the two of them. There was no love here. There was no respect, no mutual appreciation. She knew already that her boy was of a good disposition, she had to nurture that as best she could and this place—this life—was no way to do that.

By the time she had processed this, Marko had already headed for the door, cursing under his breath as he slammed the door angrily in his wake. She stood there for a few minutes, trying to absorb what had just happened, the turning of gears she just put into motion. She went back to the kitchen to the phone to call her parents. There was no way she could stay, not after the scene she had just witnessed.

In a little under an hour, Maria's father arrived to pick her and Gabriel up and take them home. All she left for Marko was a single note, stating that she could not go on like this and she was leaving.

Once they were in, the car started up and they drove off. They drove through town, taking her beloved Jamaica Way to head over onto the Southeast Expressway. The trip was silent for the most part.

As they drove past the majestic gates of the Arboretum she thought of the first time she had been there with Matt. It seemed like such a long time ago, but it really had not been so far away. She was so different now from the person she was then that she might as well be looking at another person's life.

She sighed. Such a tiny event passed her by, changing everything. She looked over to Gabriel, who was staring out his own window watching the world go by. She smiled in spite of herself; he was her whole world now. His safety and happiness had to come first, no matter what.

They exited the expressway near her parents' home, when Maria saw the sign for the local attorney's office, a sign she had seen so many times before and never paid it much thought. She offhandedly asked her father to stop there, and she got out of the vehicle, resolutely striding inside. She knew how this needed to end, and this is where she would start.

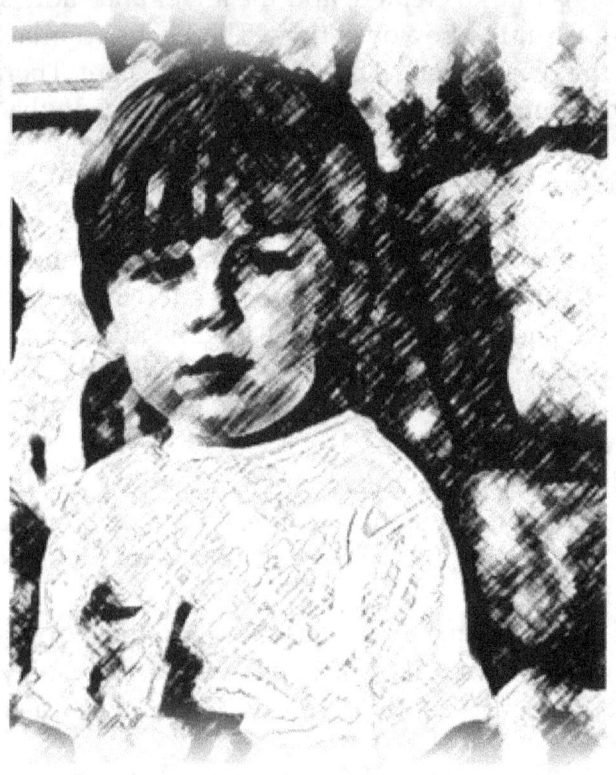

♑⚥♑⚥♑⚥♑⚥♑⚥♑⚥

"Mama Sou"

Maria came back to the apartment while Marko was out, several days later. Despite how much they had tried to fill the small apartment, the place seemed so hollow and empty under the shadows looming over her and her son. Though he was not there, Marko's presence permeated the apartment, hanging like a poisonous cloud over all the memories, good and bad, that had gathered in this place. She could almost smell the cheap wine and cigarettes on his breath just looking at his photo, and it made her stomach turn.

As she walked through the place she once called her home, she began to select things that she was going to take. There were many things she needed, dictated by necessity, but she did not see any reason to stop there. This separation marked her rift with an old life, and not everything from that life bore the taint of Marko and his lies. Those were things she wanted, fragments of times when things were better . . . no, when she thought things were better. Things had never been good, and now she understood that.

The set of dishes: too bulky, she wouldn't need them. The glasses: they would break on the drive. This book was fine, but this one he would notice was missing. She did this with every item she came by, on the way to her room. Most things were too impractical or obvious to take. She filled up her suitcase with clothes for her and Gabriel, but nothing much more was suitable to take.

She did manage to find a few photographs she still fancied, and several that were important enough to keep despite how they made her feel. But there was one she came across that she did not have the heart to take. It was a photo of Marko's father, taken not long before he died. Though she was tempted to bring it with her, she realized that it might be better to leave it here. Gabriel Senior would watch over this much more empty apartment, and maybe when he looked at it, Marko would see how disappointed his father would have been in him. He would look into his father's judging eyes, and see that he was wrong, how much he had lost in being so selfish and cruel.

In spite of herself, she smirked and shook her head. Marko would never see that; he only saw what he wanted to see.

Maria had collected all she could manage to take. In about fifteen minutes, she had reduced all of her old life to the contents of a suitcase. The rest of the things she had left were not necessary; he could keep it or sell it for all she cared. She looked over to the photo of Gabriel Senior she left behind, and whispered one last quiet goodbye to him, and prayed quietly that he would watch over her and little Gabriel in these days to come. She closed the door behind her, making her way out to her father's car where he and her baby boy were waiting for her. They drove away, to a place where she and Gabriel could be happy, where they would have light once again. Still, the further they drove, the more Maria felt that the shadows in the apartment had followed them, always clinging to the edge of her mind. It was then she realized that this darkness would not be shed easily.

♑♓♑♓♑♓♑♓♑♓

Time passed for Maria and her family in the plodding way it does while waiting. She settled back in at her parents' home, and though she felt freer and lighter without Marko there, she knew one day she would need to deal with the shadows he cast across her life. His greed and selfishness would not let her be free of him easily, she knew, and it hurt her to think that little Gabriel might one day be affected by his father's wicked ways.

The unstable situation Maria had fallen into made her unsure of what to do next. Sure, she had left Marko physically, but he was still very much a part of her life. Day after day, she was confronted with the question she did not want to answer yet: "What are you going to do about Marko?"

That was what she was waiting for; an answer.

Some days later, Marko called her at her parents house.

"Are you done visiting your parents yet?" he asked impatiently. "You need to come home soon."

Maria sighed deeply. "I'm not coming back," Maria said. After all that had happened, the note she left, all her and Gabriel's clothes missing . . . how he could have missed such an enormous clue was beyond her understanding. He just did not seem to think she was strong enough to leave the life he gave her. It was just one more thing Marko was in denial over.

He was silent at first. "What do you mean?"

"I've been to an attorney, I filed for divorce a few days ago."

"Why would you do that, honey?"

"We aren't good for each other, Marko," Maria said, trying to be as sensitive as possible. "It's not going to work out, we need to end this."

"No, we can make this work, it will be fine," Marko said, irritation clear in his tone.

"I tried to, Marko. I can't ignore your 'disappearances', your discretions. I won't. This is not the life I want, and certainly not the life I want for my son."

"Listen, you stupid woman, you are coming back and that's that!"

Maria sighed despite his rage. There had been a chance that she had remorse for her actions when this conversation started; that was not going to happen now. Somehow, she had fooled herself into thinking that it would not come to this. "You have no respect, Marko. For yourself or for me. It's over."

Marko sighed this time. "You know what? Fine! You can have your silly little divorce. It's fine with me. I'll be by in an hour to pick up Gabriel."

Maria's heart strained for a moment. "Oh, no you won't."

"He is my son!"

"You will not take Gabriel, end of story. No court in the land would ever grant you custody. You leave all the time, for absolutely no reason for days at a time and with nothing to show for it. I have several witnesses who will testify to that, as well. You won't have him just to leave him somewhere while you go drinking!"

After several more minutes of arguing, Marko vowed to her that she would never get her divorce, and that Gabriel would end up with him no matter what. Maria was not scared; she knew she was right, and no amount of his pestering could change that.

Not for a lack of trying, though. Many times, Marko would come and try to bring her back to him. If Maria was unstable throughout this ordeal, Marko could only be described as a man on the brink. One moment, they would be discussing things rationally, in moments that almost made Maria feel selfish. But seemingly out of nowhere, his tone would become vicious and cold, and he would make threats that he thought she could not hear. Those moments solidified her resolve to stay on her path; his cruelty was crystallizing Maria's vision, and each cold threat and poor excuse made that crystal even clearer.

Maria had made her choice, and would not be swayed. Marko's desperation became clear as he started to strike at her family.

His lies were not going to work on Maria anymore, but the rest of her family was not so deaf to his words. He visited her relatives, aunts and uncles, her grandmother, anyone who would listen. He fed them his sob story, how Maria had left him because she had abruptly decided she did not want to be married anymore, how she had used him—*how she used him*—to get what she wanted and left when she had it. He told this story with crocodile tears in his eyes, and they believed his words and his tears.

Even Maria's parents were not immune to the unspoken threats Marko had made. Though they did not believe his stories, they said nothing about Maria's situation to anyone else. They had no wish to draw Marko's ire, so they never spoke to anyone about his misdeeds. It was also embarrassing that their oldest daughter had married such a disrespectful and dreadful man.

On top of that, the idea of divorce was not very acceptable in Portugal or Greece, and her parents and family were still heavily in that mindset. Marko took advantage of that to continually paint her in a bad light.

When his constant prattling had worn them down, sometimes Maria's parents would try to convince her to be "reasonable," to them it was simply that divorce was not acceptable, and she had plenty of friends that had been married and quite content even if they were not completely happy. Maria, however, knew that all of these friends of hers had plenty of partners in their time, but somehow were still "respectable women" because they were married and did not get divorced.

Divorce seemed to be a dirtier word than whore to her parents, and she had no idea why. They whispered it during conversations as though they were invoking the devil. Maria at least knew what she wanted from marriage. There had to be love, respect, and understanding. Happiness was central to what marriage meant, not one bad choice she would now always regret. She told this to her parents' startled faces, retorting that she had only been with one man ever, and their pleading was not going to make the broken relationship work, by what reasoning did getting a lawful divorce make her the unreasonable one?

Her parents left the matter alone after that.

Still, Marko was persistent in his attempts to persuade Maria. He came to her parents' house to try and convince her on many occasions.

"You are never, *never* going to get this divorce, do you hear me?" He told her during one visit, standing in the doorway imperiously.

"I will not let you stop me this time, Marko," she said, barring him from the rest of the house. "You've hurt me, and that's enough, but I won't let you hurt our son."

"He is my son," Marko growled, "You won't keep him."

"He is my son too," Maria said defiantly. "He deserves to live with someone who loves him, not with someone who will just treat him like a possession and use him like a tool."

Marko's face became dark red. He took two steps toward Maria. She stood her ground, motionless, their faces almost touching. He said in Greek in a very low, threatening tone, "Maria, I swear to God, if you go through with this, I will cut you into little pieces."

His words, his tone, and the barbaric language startled her. Maria backed up instinctively, which attracted her mother's attention from the other room. "Is something wrong?" she asked as she came up to them. "What did he just say?"

Without thinking, and still shocked, Maria blurted out the translation of what Marko had said. At first he seemed ready to attack her. But Maria's mother would have none of it.

"Listen to me," she roared at him. "We'll have no more of your threats and lies in this house! Now go, leave, before I cook you alive and chop *you* into pieces!"

Marko backed away, visibly cowed by the fury of the older woman. Maria's mother reached past her and slammed the door, locking it and storming off back to the other room, taking Maria by the hand and muttering angry things under her breath in Portuguese.

Maria understood the power of motherly instincts, but watching it play out before her, outside of her own actions, held up a mirror to what she had done. Her mother's violent outburst was protective, trying to save her child from something dangerous. Just like Maria had done.

Though he had been denied there, Marko's tricks were numerous and insidious. Some days later, he called Maria at her parent's house.

"I'm coming by again," he said evenly. "I want to talk to you."

"I don't want to see you again, Marko." Maria told him. "You aren't welcome here anymore."

"I don't care, I still want to talk you. I've been speaking with your aunt Sylvia, and she agrees with me."

"No, she doesn't," Maria said, irritated. "She would never agree with you."

"She does," Marko said. "Your cousins think you should come back to me as well,"

"You stay away from them, Marko," Maria shouted defensively. She hated the idea that her family would agree with Marko and not her. They had not even heard her side of things, how could they just trust him like that?

"They think you are being a silly child, and that you should grow up and do as you are told," Marko continued, ceaselessly. "Ahh, but they are amazing women, your cousins. We got along very well."

"Marko, stop," Maria demanded, angry tears forming in her eyes.

"One of them cried for me while I was there, pitying me and telling me how sorry she was because of you. She gave me quite a nice kiss as well—"

Maria hung up, slamming the receiver down. The nerve of him, to be so bold with her family! She and her cousins were very close, and near the same age as well. How could they think such things of her?

He had to have been lying, she told herself. There was simply no way, *no way* that this could be true. Her cousins loved her, and would never say such things about her. Or would they? Surely they could see that Marko was lying, couldn't they? She wiped the tears from her eyes, and kept repeating to herself how much of a liar he was, but in the back of her mind doubt nagged at her, because once upon a time, she had believed those lies as well.

A few minutes later she heard a car pull into the driveway, and her mother yelled to her, "Maria! What is Marko doing here?"

Maria charged to the front door, looking out to indeed see that Marko had parked out in front of the house. Her rage was beginning to mount in a terrible way. She specifically told him not to come here. He was overstepping his bounds, as usual, but she was sick and tired of his attitude. After saying the things he said on the phone, he dared to come to her home and pester her further?

She was fed up. This was too much.

"Maria, just who I wanted to see," Marko said casually, still in the car with a smirk on his face.

"Get the hell out of here, you son of a bitch!" Maria screamed at him. "Get out or I will call the police, I swear to God!"

"I just want to talk," Marko said quietly, still nonchalant despite her outburst. "Come into the car, please. I'm tired of fighting, and I miss you and Gabriel. Just a few minutes, that's all I ask.

"You've said enough over the phone, all of it hurtful!"

"Just give me one chance."

Maria started to doubt what she was feeling. This could all have been a misunderstanding, however unlikely that seemed. Still, she had to give him the benefit of the doubt. She knew she was going to regret it, but something about the way he was being quiet and reasonable made her feel almost sorry for him. She got into the car, still skeptical despite her compromise.

"What do you have to say for yourself?" she asked, much more calmly, arms crossed.

"We both know this is a silly argument." Marko said, still pleasant. "You will come back in the end because it's the right thing, for you and for Gabriel."

"No, there's nothing right about how you treat us," Maria said, feeling more than a little betrayed here.

"But what about you cousins and aunt? They understand how I feel. I wish you were more like them," he said, trying to hide his smug smile.

"My cousins and aunt are idiots!" Maria shouted, losing her temper to rage. "Anyone who listens to you is a goddamn idiot!"

"But Sylvia really thinks you should think about it."

"I don't care what Aunt Sylvia thinks; they don't know what you put me through!" Maria was now completely enraged. What was he even doing here? Why play with her emotions and torment her like this? Her trust had been violated again, and he had just wanted to bring up her cousins and aunt to get her riled.

Confused and frustrated, she got out of the car and slammed the door. "Now get out of here!"

Marko shrugged coldly and rolled up the window, started the car and left. Maria stood for a moment, confused. He gave up way too easily that time, as though he wanted things to go this way. Why did he not fight back this time?

Still, she sighed in relief. He was gone for now, before he could do much more than irritate her. That was an unsurpassable blessing at this point.

A few days passed, quietly and without incidence from Marko. These breaks in insanity were the closest thing Maria got to spending time like a normal person. She spent much of the time she had like this with Gabriel, who was speaking well, and even reading some short words now. Sometimes she would read to him, other times, he would ask to read to her and make up the story as she flipped the pages. She wanted times like this to be what was normal, not the other way around. Her life felt so backwards, all because of one cruel man.

Then, one afternoon, Maria's mother came to her after talking on the phone.

"Maria, Sylvia just called," She said. "You said some nasty things about them?"

"What?" Maria said. "No, I didn't."

"They said that Marko . . ."

"I thought you told them he was lying! You said you told them!"

"I did," her mother said. "But they said Marko had a cassette tape, he played it for them, and you said something terrible, that you don't care what they think and that they are stupid."

"I . . ." Maria was dumbstruck. That bastard had recorded their conversation! He got her all riled up and pushed all the right buttons just to make her say terrible things.

And just like a child, she bumbled into his trap and played right into his hands.

"I didn't mean it . . ." she said quietly. "I was mad. He told me they agreed with him, sympathized with him! I felt betrayed, I didn't mean what I said!"

"I know, but that's not what they think." Maria's mother turned to leave. "I told her not to call again, don't worry."

Tears welled up in Maria's eyes. How did this help him? What did he have to gain from making her family mad at her? Did it just make him happy to see her suffer? That seemed obvious, but they had had nothing to do with this, why did he have to drag them into their fight? He clearly did not care who he hurt, as long as he thought he could get an advantage out of it.

A few stressful days later, Maria's Uncle Tom came to visit. Saying he had business in town and decided to stop by, Maria was happy at first for the welcome distraction, but soon after, Tom asked to talk to her privately.

"What's the matter?" Maria asked.

"I wanted to ask you how your marriage was going," Tom said.

"Oh . . . it's really not too bad." Maria said, trying to avoid saying anything until she was ready to tell everyone.

"Well, I heard you were going through a rough time," Tom told her. "It's nothing to be ashamed of, it happens to the best of us."

"What are you saying, uncle?" Maria asked.

"I'm just saying, it would be a good idea to think things through, give it some time. Divorce is a serious thing, you know."

Realization dawned on Maria as he spoke. "Uncle, did Marko talk to you?"

"He did, but maybe he's right," Tom said. "He seemed pretty distraught, he was even crying. He's very worried about you . . ."

"Tom!" Maria's mother shouted. She had apparently overheard what they were talking about. "What are you saying to Maria?"

"I'm just trying to help," Tom said.

"She knows what she's doing, you leave her alone. You don't have the whole story," Maria's mother said.

"I'm just looking out for her," Tom said. "Marko seemed thin and sickly, it might help him to be with his family."

"I don't care how he looked, he can't be trusted!" Maria's mother yelled. She was visibly starting to tear up. "You have no idea what's going on, so stop butting into her business!"

"She might regret this . . ." Tom started to say, but Maria's mother would have none of it.

"Get out right now!" She screeched, now full on crying. "You are not welcome here; no one in this family will tell my daughter how to live her life!"

Tom was rushed out of the house rather quickly, but Maria still felt as though all parts of her life were being violated. There was a boundary that Marko had crossed somewhere, that made her feel unsafe in all of her life now. One of the reasons she left him was one of the reasons he was so threatening now: without a job, Marko had all the free time in the world to weave together his schemes. Were there no lengths he would not go to, no family members he wouldn't turn against her?

Little did she know; that question would soon be answered.

A week later, Maria went to her grandmother's house with her mother and Gabriel. She started worrying that Marko had somehow gotten to her, and she was the last person she wanted to lose to Marko's wiles. She just wanted to know that she was alright.

Maria's grandmother was quite enamored with little Gabriel, and was absolutely delighted every time she saw him. She always gave him three or four kisses, with machine gun-like speed, on each cheek. She always followed up with the classic cheek pinch, cooing and saying how adorable he was. Gabriel didn't care for that at all, but she was always ready to win him over again with sweets, like chocolate chip cookies or ginger snaps.

This time, things went much the same. She did her little routine with Gabriel, and when he started pouting she handed him a big chocolate chip cookie, and he toddled off. But instead of being her regular, cheerful self, she just quietly went about making tea for them. Maria felt that something was not quite right, but was not sure how to broach the subject.

She looked around. All seemed to be well; her father and Gabriel were sitting in the living room watching television, flipping through the channels casually. Everything in the kitchen, where she and her mother were sitting, seemed to be fine. Nothing stood out to her as amiss; her grandmother just seemed to be acting funny.

"So how are you doing?" Maria asked, hoping that it was just nothing.

"Me? I am perfectly fine," she said. "I am quite worried about you though."

"What do you mean?" Maria asked.

She brought over ginger snaps and tea, sat down and said, "I spoke to Marko the other day."

In a way Maria was relieved. She did not have to broach the topic; her grandmother already knew. She just had to share her side of things with her and there would not be any problems.

She reached out and put her hand on her grandmother's hand, ready to explain everything, but her grandmother reached out and put her hand on Maria's before she could say anything.

"I know it is scary to leave your family, Maria," she said. "I felt much the same, when I moved away with your grandfather. But you are married now; you have to be responsible to your family. Your husband needs you, so stop being a child, and go with him to Greece!"

Maria had no words; the shock of what she just heard had taken them. Nothing was left but a disappointed pit in her heart. How could she have said such a horrible thing? She did not even wait to hear her side, this was the only way it could be to her.

While Maria struggled to form her thoughts into words, Maria's mother tried to defend her. "Mother, you don't have the whole story . . ."

Her grandmother cut her off with a wave of her hand, signifying that she did not want to hear any more. She stood up and walked to the stove, where the kettle was whistling. Maria's mother started fuming angrily, signifying that a fight was about to start.

Maria could not bear it. The thought of yet another part of their family being broken apart was too much for her. She stood up abruptly, startling the other two.

"Stop," she said. "Just stop before it happens again! No more fighting, I can't take it!"

Maria turned to her grandmother, looking her straight in the eye. She surely was thrown off by Maria's sudden outburst, but seemed to expect her to argue still. Instead, Maria walked up to her and threw her arms around her in a tight hug.

"Please Vovo, just listen to my side of things," Maria said softly. "All I ask is that you hear me out before you decided which of us to support. You know I love you and would never lie to you . . . you must know that. Please let me talk, and I'll answer any questions and tell you anything you want to know after, okay?"

Her grandmother was still as Maria stepped away, her expression was that of shock, but she was still composed. After a tense moment of held breath, she let out a conciliatory sigh. "Alright, then. Let's sit and talk."

Maria wasted no time in explaining exactly how she felt. How she had been treated by Marko, how hard the decision had been to make, the moment when Gabriel was hugging his father's knees, begging him not to fight. As she spoke, she relived it all, and all the emotion she was trying to keep down flooded to the surface. It spilled over into her mother and grandmother, who shared her tears as she told her sorry tale.

When she was done, her grandmother told her exactly what Marko had said when she met him. He had made it sound as though she was being a stupid child and clinging to her family irresponsibly. He had colored her a selfish brat that did not want to do her duty as a wife. In his story, he was the victim, and Maria was the one ruining everything.

"I can see now that it's completely backwards," her grandmother said. "He's such a coward, trying to use me like this. He'll get what he deserves, you'll see Maria!"

By the time they left her grandmother's house, all of them had shed quite a few tears, but they were all better off for it. It was exactly the opposite of how she feared it would turn out, and that made Maria happy, even if it was a minor victory it meant so very much to her right now.

A short time later, she found out that her grandmother was still in contact with Marko. When she asked her about it, she smiled wryly. "He's not the only one who can play this game. Think of me as your spy, Maria. I just want to see if he will let anything slip that we can use. He thinks he's using me, but I can act just as well as him—maybe even better! Just leave it to me, I'll give a little of what he wants to hear, and maybe I'll get some juicy bits for you to use."

As much as Maria appreciated her grandmother's willingness to help, she wondered if stooping to his level was really the best solution. She soon realized that prudence was going to be the key to winning this fight. It seemed the old saying was true; all is fair in love and war.

♑♓♑♓♑♓♑♓♑♓♑♓

A small but very important victory came to Maria sometime later. After her lawyer had presented the evidence and gotten all their witnesses to testify, she was awarded complete custody of Gabriel. Marko would still be able to see Gabriel, but he needed to get Maria's permission and a court appointed chaperone. She now had legal confirmation that Gabriel was to be with her.

When Marko found out he was absolutely livid. He railed and raged, causing a gigantic impotent fit. Maria felt almost sorry for him, but how could he be responsible for a child when he acted so childish?

Things started to take a bit of a turn for the better after that. Maria felt more justified now that she had the court's ruling on her side. The court had given her full custody, making her feel completely reasonable in her actions, despite what Marko had to say. It gave her a boost of confidence when dealing with Marko, who was hardly deterred by the words of a judge. His persistence was almost admirable, even if it was manically obsessive. He still demanded that she return his son to him, and for a while all she had to do was say no.

But one final time, he came to her place and threatened with force if she did not give Gabriel back, and she warned him, "If you so much as come near me, I will call the police, and you'll never see him again!"

That gave him pause. The slow shift in his demeanor told her that he understood that she was not bluffing. He backed off, still angry despite his realization. "This isn't over," he said. With that he stormed out, but Maria could not help but feel that he was blustering, wasting breath in an attempt to convince her that he still had a leg to stand on in this argument.

The next few days were rather quiet. Maria normally got angry calls from him at least once a day, but since she had warned him, he had not called once.

However, he did eventually call. She completely expected him to continue being aggressive, and was almost curious to see what new ways he would try to manipulate her.

Instead, she heard him say something she did not expect.

"I miss Gabriel very much. May I take him to the park?"

She hesitated. "I have to call the court and tell them to send a chaperone, first."

His response took a moment. "That's fine. I won't be long. I'll be over tomorrow afternoon to pick him up, alright?"

"Yes, alright," she replied. "If there's a problem with the chaperone, I'll let you know."

After they hung up, Maria almost was more unsettled than she would have been if he had called to yell at her. Was he sincere in his change of heart, or was this the beginning of some cunning ploy? Still, she picked the phone back up to arrange a chaperone, though his sudden attitude shift weighed on her mind.

The next day, Marko came by, and waited patiently until the chaperone showed up. They then went to the park, leaving Maria to ponder whether or not Marko would do something desperate once he was alone with the boy.

However, Marko and Gabriel came back with the chaperone, both of them in high spirits. Marko left soon after, thanking Maria for letting him have time with his son.

"Would it be okay if we did this again soon?" he asked, hope in his voice and in his eyes.

Maria had no choice but to agree, or her heart would not be able to take it. He was clearly broken by this ordeal, probably as much as she was. He was finally playing by the rules, and his attitude was the best she had ever experienced from him.

Over the next few weeks, Marko came to see Gabriel several times. He took him to different places, like the park and the playground, and one time they even went to one of those photo booths and took a bunch of pictures. All of this without fuss concerning the chaperone. His compliance made her confused and relieved, something so strange and alien a concept as his patience giving her pause for concern, but the fact that he was cooperating was so welcome a change that she could scarcely believe it was for real. The worst of it was that Gabriel had enjoyed it so much that he wanted to go back right away. Nothing pained her more than the guilt she felt when she saw them enjoying things together, she had kept them apart for so long, but this is all she was keeping them from. Why did he never do these things when they had been together?

It hurt so much to remember what things were like before . . . or rather, how she imagined things were before. She had to keep telling herself that it had all been her delusion, but seeing Marko and her son together almost made her feel like they were a family not long ago.

It was around September when Marko mentioned he would like to take Gabriel to Boston Garden to see the circus. He wistfully told her how he had gone with his own father when he was younger, about all the good things he remembered from those times, and how he wanted Gabriel to have that experience as well.

Every time he brought it up it made Maria's heart ache. All it made her want was a normal family life, one where her son could make all kinds of nice memories, not just ones where papa was angry or mama was crying. She knew it was not going to happen, but deep down she wanted to believe it could.

Each time they had the conversation Marko would finish it with a longing sigh. It seemed like he was just trying to make memories with Gabriel, something they would have to remember so that he was not missing completely from his son's life. It touched Maria that he was being so thoughtful of his son, and she wanted to agree to let them go. But an unexpected twist was brought up the next time they talked about it.

"You want to take him without a chaperone?" Maria repeated incredulously.

"Yes," Marko said. "I don't want some other person there, watching my every move and making my son think I can't be trusted."

"No, Marko," Maria said, adamantly. "These visits have been good up till now, you need to stick to it."

"No, please!" he pleaded, practically going to his knees. "I need this, Maria, I really need this! It would . . . I would be so grateful, just so happy to not have a chaperone this one time. Just this once, never again! Think of how much Gabriel would like spending an afternoon with his father, no one else around to make it awkward for us!"

Maria just wanted Gabriel to be happy. She almost wanted to say she wanted to go with them. But she stopped herself at that, it would be the worst lie she could make her son believe. Marko was being so agreeable now, though. It was a breath of fresh air compared to the usual aggressive, egocentric man that forced her away from him. She actually wanted to trust him, just this one time.

Would this one time be so bad?

"Alright, Marko," she said. "Just this once! You need to be back as soon as it's over!"

"Thank you, Maria," he said, a look of joy on his face. "This will be the best for Gabriel, I promise."

From that day on, Marko brought up the trip whenever he came to see Gabriel. His enthusiasm was quite contagious to Gabriel, who became genuinely excited about this trip he was about to take. Every day he had questions about what was at the circus, and it seemed every answer was more amazing than he had anticipated.

The day of the circus, Gabriel was hopping up and down with excitement. Maria and her relatives all made a big deal about the adventure this day had in store for him. To see him so genuinely happy was such a thrill that it was hard not to keep telling him stories. They filled his head with thoughts of lions, clowns, trapeze artists, not to mention the huge elephants he would see. All the attention further fueled his adventurous spirit, and when it was time for him to go, he was giddy with curiosity. Maria hugged him goodbye and gave him a kiss, only telling him to have fun before Marko arrived and picked him up. Maria watched as the car drove off, hoping they did indeed have a good day.

After this, she felt she could give the three of them another chance. Maybe things could be different. Marko seemed to appreciate his son after having him taken away for so long, perhaps he understood what he was missing. There was a smile on Maria's face that she could not explain to her family as she went back into the house. Hope had slipped in once more, even if it was only a little.

Later, however, worry started to creep in, pushing that hope down into a dark, cold corner. Marko had said he would be back with Gabriel around seven o'clock, but that clearly was not the case because it was eight now and she had not received word from him. She thought perhaps he had simply not estimated correctly, but something nagging deep inside told her that was not true. Had something happened? Did the car break down? Was there an accident?

Her Aunt Elena and Uncle Samuel were visiting her parents that evening. Maria noticed their conversation had become sparse and quiet, almost to a whisper, the more Maria looked out the window. Her aunt kept telling her to relax, suggesting that they had stopped off for an ice cream after the circus. Maria did not respond to her, and no more comments from anyone were heard.

Maria paced back and forth by the phone, worried sick and just waiting to hear something. A call finally came around nine o'clock, but it was a voice she did not recognize.

"There is a letter in the mailbox outside," the voice said. "It will explain everything." After that was said, the phone was hung up and all Maria heard was the dial tone and her heart pounding loudly.

She rushed outside as millions of panicked scenarios ran through her head. She reached the mailbox and sure enough, a single unmarked envelope was inside. As she picked it up, the reality of her situation set in, and her heart pounded louder and louder. She brought it back inside and opened it, revealing a plain looking letter, typed up on a typewriter.

"Maria, do not come looking for Gabriel. He is out of the country by now, you will not see him again."

PART IV

The Edge

Maria's entire body felt numb, like the worst winter storm had covered her in ice. When she felt as though she might fall, she reached out for a chair so she could hold herself up. She wanted to cry, to scream, but all that would pass through her lips was a very soft "Oh my God," again and again.

While her body was failing, her mind was racing. There was no way she could let this happen. She could fall apart later; she needed to do something, anything to save her son now!

She forced herself to move, taking one agonizingly slow step at a time over to the phone as she wobbled from side to side. She grabbed the receiver and forced her hand to dial the number of Tom Sullivan, her lawyer.

"Hello?"

"Marko took him! He took Gabriel! They could be anywhere, please help!" Maria managed to choke out as loud as her voice would let her.

"Maria? Oh my god . . . Just wait, I'm going to make a few calls and then I'll be over in a minute."

Tom arrived at her mother's house a short while later. He explained that he had called a judge to get a warrant for Marko's arrest, and also the Sheriff's office to have them cover the airport. He came over because he needed to ask her some questions the authorities would want to know.

She was worried at first that he would ask how Marko had been allowed to take Gabriel unsupervised, but strangely he had avoided the question. Something told her he already had guessed what was going on. By the manner in which he circled around that aspect, she suspected that he already knew that she blamed herself for the whole thing.

And why should she not? After all, it was her stupidity that let Marko go without the supervision he was supposed to have. She had been so naïve, to let herself believe that things were starting to change, that it was getting just a little bit better. Blinded by hope, she gave Marko just a little bit of leeway. But he had betrayed her. *She* had betrayed herself by trusting him, trusting a man that had not a few short months ago threatened to kill her over wanting a divorce.

Why did she let this happen?

She would not let it happen again. She vowed then to never believe in the goodness of humanity. She was done being naïve, assuming that others had good intentions. People needed to prove themselves first, and she would not have it any other way. She could not afford to be caught off guard by anyone for any reason, everyone would have to earn her trust.

As soon as he had all the information he needed, Tom left, reassuring her that they would do whatever they could to get her son back. He promised that Marko and Gabriel's faces would be all over the airport in an hour, and that the police would be questioning everyone who looked even slightly similar.

His words gave Maria a little hope, but somewhere deep inside she felt that the damage had already been done. She truly hoped that they would catch Marko before he could get away, but it had already been so long.

Around midnight, she received another call from Tom. He told her that they had no luck finding Marko and Gabriel at the airport, he had likely already gone. The despair she already felt grew deeper. How could this be happening?

The next day, Maria called all her friends, everyone in the family she could think of, trying to find out if they knew anything. She spent hours on the phone, desperate to learn more. But with every call, every negative response, every condolence, she lost another sliver of hope.

Soon she began to doubt the sincerity of the people who contacted her. How many of them might have known ahead of time? Family had betrayed her before, what was to say that others would not as well? If that was the case, how could they possibly condone kidnapping of such a small child from his mother? These conspiracy theories whirled around in her mind time and time again when she talked to people. Eventually her heart hardened, and any genuine thing that anyone told her was lost among every perceived lie and disdain she heard.

After she exhausted all her options and contacts that might have known what had happened, it finally hit her. She had no idea where her son was, and might not ever see him again. The panic washed up on her like an ocean wave, cold and stark. She started to shake tremulously, tears rolling down her cheeks. She was sobbing and weeping so profusely that she could barely hear her parents as they tried to console her. It was not life now, without her son it was just existence, and such an existence was nothing she wanted a part of. The only thing that kept her going was the off chance that someone would find Gabriel, and he would need her then. But for now, all was chaos, descending madness. Nothing made sense to her right now, it seemed like all hope had been lost.

It had been hopeless from the start. Maria learned (albeit much later) that Marko had never taken Gabriel to the circus to begin with. Marko had left directly for the airport as soon as he was out of sight of Maria's parents place. He then had taken a flight over to the west coast and stayed with relatives, under the guise of "just visiting."

It was not as though they had helped him knowing though. His cousin had actually asked where she was, and he lied to them as well, saying she was not feeling well, and he would have brought her if not for her health. They trusted him, as she did, thus he was allowed to carry out his scheme.

From the west coast, he got an international flight back to Greece. He got a passport for himself and Gabriel by using the pictures he had taken from the photo booth just weeks ago. Something Maria had thought was just a frivolous outing turned out to be a cornerstone of his master plan. He had planned this much longer than she had given him credit for.

Every feigned emotion and false word came back to haunt her. All the emotions of sympathy and doubt were thrust back at her like knives, flashing with cold and bitter loathing. He had played her like a song, and she had sung the harmony.

His very existence was cruel to her.

While he was absconding with their son, Maria was falling deep into depression. She reached the point at which she was too tired to cry. Her tears and soul were dried, parched from caring and feeling. The amount she was eating was getting less all the time, eventually she reached a point where her diet consisted primarily of coffee . . . and cigarettes. She had tried so hard to quit, keeping her son in mind, but now the one or two sporadic weekly cigarettes had become a daily need, a mindless vice.

Most of the time she wanted to bury herself in the covers of her bed, not sure if she would ever come out again. She moved from her room into the basement, isolating herself from the memories that were crushing her spirit. Every voice and laugh she heard was a stinging reminder of the life she could have had. Resentment piled up within her, watching others move on with their lives and forget—how *dare* they—while she was stuck in the moment she opened that letter.

She wanted to wake up and find Gabriel in his room every day, but every day she was disappointed. She wanted to be able to move on, to make her life right again. But how could she—how *dare* she even want it—when she might never know what happened to her son. The pain she felt was unbearable, if God was merciful there could not be a pain worse than this.

At night she would lie in bed wondering what went wrong. There must be something she could do to change things. She was brought up in a religious household, and believed that God had a plan. That plan had an answer for everything, a reason for all the madness. But how could this be His plan for her? She had lived a good life, did what she could, tried to help others and do what was right. So why was this happening to her; why was she being punished? She would just shake her head, thinking, "What did I do to deserve this?"

Marko had turned her into a victim, something she never thought would happen in her life. She had stood up to him and he hurt her in the worst way he possibly could. She hoped now, she *had* to hope, that someone or something would show her how to be strong enough to endure this so she could get him back. How was she supposed to do this on her own?

During this time began the court hearing for her divorce. She knew, somewhere deep down, that going to these hearings would be the best way to get Gabriel back sooner. But she could not bring herself to face the realities at hand. If she went to the hearings, she would have to do it knowing that she would have to face Marko in some way or another. She could not do it. So whenever Tom called to tell her about the court date, she would tell him to postpone. It had to happen, but she knew she could not do it now.

This state of affairs continued to decline for some time. Her mood became darker as her frustration and anguish mounted, her energy dwindled, and her nights became longer. She dreaded opening her eyes every morning, there was no way this version of her life was better than the oblivion of sleep. From time to time, Maria's mother would invite over other members of the family, just to see if they could bring Maria out of her shell—out of the basement—a little. But time and time again, she refused to even engage with company. She just stayed in the basement, wanting to shut out the world and everything in it.

The saddest thing was that she wanted to change the most, but her mind would not let her. The darkness was a comfort where the light made the truth hurt more. She hurt sometimes when there was no reason to feel pain. She would lie in bed during the day, breathing too loudly and trying to fill the room with her breath. She was sick in a way medicine could not help.

In the hours she spent alone, she could only relive the day it happened again and again, trying to understand why it happened. She shouted at the dark, angry at invisible people for invisible reasons, calling herself stupid and foolish. And still her mind tortured her on the simple fact that she trusted the wrong person, and knew it the whole time.

The worst was that she found she could not trust anything anymore. Her mind shut out anything that offered even the semblance of relief or joy. Friendly faces could be shunning her behind her back. Encouraging words were always assumed to be wrong, wrong enough to mean the opposite of what was said. Her own words had double meanings to her; she doubted the truth of anything that she said. If she could not trust herself, who could she trust?

One day, her mother came down to the basement to talk. Maria told her to come in, but did not bother getting out of her bed.

"Sweetie, why don't you change into some other clothes so I can wash your pajamas?" she asked softly, doing her daily due diligence in trying to engage with Maria in any way.

"I don't feel like it," Maria said.

"Oh, come on, they'll be nice and warm out of the dryer," Maria's mother said. "You can change right back into them when they're out. It's not healthy to stay in the same clothes all the time."

Grumbling, Maria agreed. Her mother also convinced her to take a shower and clean up, since she was changing anyway. After she had washed, changed, and dried her hair, she sat wrapped in her oversized robe in the living room to wait for her pajamas to be ready again.

Her mother came into the room, saying that they dryer was acting up again, and it would be a while before her bedclothes were done. Sighing, Maria nodded. She had plenty of time to wait after all.

"While we're waiting, why don't we go for a drive?" Maria's mother suggested. "Just a nice, relaxing trip to get some fresh air and a change of scenery."

Maria finished her cup of coffee, shrugging noncommittally. It was too much trouble to argue. She threw on a shirt and a pair of jeans, along with a belt. Her clothes got looser every time she needed to get dressed nowadays. In short order, she was ushered into the car before she even had a chance to change her mind.

At first she did not mind. It was a change of pace, but did not really have much of an effect on her. Some melancholy song played on the radio, something she recognized but was not sure who played it or what it was called. Fall colors were on display; bright oranges, yellows, and reds flashed in place of cool green whenever they passed foliage. It was by all accounts a beautiful fall day, and Maria could not care less.

Eventually she noticed they were getting deeper into town, and by the time she thought to ask why, her mother had pulled over next to a small retail store, one Maria had been to many times.

"Ah, just on time," she said, rather satisfied. "Come on, let's go."

"Where are we going?" Maria asked.

"Right inside, to the service desk," her mother said, rather matter-of-factly. "There's a lady there who'll let you know when the supervisor is ready for the interview."

"What interview?" Maria said, completely confused.

"Your interview," her mother explained. "Just a stocking job, nothing serious, but it's something."

"When . . ."

"I applied for it last week, for you," her mother said as they got out of the car . . . "I heard back from them yesterday, and they requested you for an interview."

"I didn't want this," Maria protested. There was no way she was going to go through with this, no matter how much forethought her mother had put into this. However, her mother was having none of it.

"You've got to get back on your feet, dear," she said, holding her hand and tugging her gently toward the entrance. "It's hard, I know. But eventually, you've got to build your life back up. This is a pretty good start; it will keep you occupied so you don't waste away in the basement. You wanted to be independent from Marko, so you have to learn to support yourself," she looked her in the eye and added, "and Gabriel, once you have him back."

Maria's heart struggled not to burst with emotion. Inspired by her mother's gesture, she stopped resisting her mother's encouraging tugs accompanied her into the building. She had her interview, which went splendidly, and she was informed that she would start her new position in two weeks.

She was quite pleased with herself, for a few days. She even brought herself to spend time outside her room or basement for a few hours every day. But slowly doubt began to creep back into her mind. She had guilt for anything that made her feel even a little bit good. She questioned whether or not she deserved to feel good about anything yet. She still found herself constantly thinking of what happened with Gabriel, about what could be happening to him right now. The thought never left her mind, it just made itself known at the most unexpected times. At work, at home, walking to open the fridge to get cream for her tea, getting a glass of water from the tap, picking up a magazine from the coffee table, it persisted. Her line of thinking progressed; if she failed to look after her child, how could she be trusted with a job?

They day after Maria fell victim to her old moping her mother came to see her.

"Maria, can you do me a favor?"

Maria shrugged. "I suppose."

"It isn't much dear. All you have to do is answer the door. I'm expecting a delivery, and need someone to receive it while I'm out."

"Oh, alright," Maria said. That was all? She would have done that much without being asked.

"Thank you dear, it means a lot," she said, leaving her be after that.

Her mother went out on her errands, and Maria passed the time reading as she waited. A few hours later, she heard the doorbell ring. She went to open the door, but noticed through the window that there was no delivery truck. Instead there was a car with the writing "student driver" on it.

The man at the front door greeted her pleasantly, introducing himself as a driving instructor. He told her that he had some lessons for Maria, they were already paid for and all she had to do was get in the car and they could start.

"I didn't ask for driving lessons," she told him.

He shrugged. "All I know is that someone paid for them, and told me to come to this address and find Maria. Do you know how to drive?" Maria shook her head. "Well, why not learn how? It's paid for anyway."

Maria suspected that this was all her mother's doing once more. At first she was upset, almost angry, at her mother's constant interference in her life. Still, she understood her reasoning. Her mother felt powerless right now, unable to change the horrible events that had befallen her family, and she did this because it was the right thing for her daughter to do. Maria had to learn to take care of herself, and this was one more step toward that. It was already paid for, so why not?

"How long will it take?"

"First lesson might take an hour, the next few probably won't take so long."

"The next few?"

"Yes, this is a series of four lessons, over two weeks."

"But I start work in two weeks."

"Well, then, I guess we better get started," he suggested. "The sooner we get started, the sooner you'll be able to drive yourself to work."

Maria smiled in spite of herself. Her mother was obviously trying to encourage her to be more independent, so she set her up to take these lessons. She was honestly touched by her mother's efforts, she clearly believed that Maria deserved better than the punishment she forced upon herself. This was just another step toward normalcy for her, and her mother was making sure she made it.

"I guess if it's already paid for . . ."

"Splendid! Just climb into the driver's seat and we'll get started!"

Maria took to the lessons like a natural, impressing her instructor by the end of the session. He told her that she would have no problems getting her license by the end of the lessons.

Driving made Maria really feel confident. She felt as though she finally had a handle on something, even if it was just driving around. But it was a start, just the kind of start she needed.

The boost of confidence proved to be helpful when she finished her lessons and started her new job. She no longer felt like she was unqualified or inferior, rather she felt like she was ready to try. She still was not fully confident, but it was no longer in her mind that she would definitely fail. She was able to give herself a chance again.

A short time after she had started her job, she got another visit from Tom. He was waiting for her after she came home from work one afternoon, sitting with her mother at the kitchen table.

"Maria, it's good to see you again," he said, motioning for her to sit down with them. "How are you feeling?"

"Better, I suppose," she answered, pulling up a chair to the table. "Is this about a hearing?"

"You really need to come to court. This is getting very serious."

The old feelings of anxiety and depression came back to her. "No, I don't think I am ready yet."

"You can't keep avoiding this, if you ever want to see your son again!" he told her firmly. "What can I say more? I simply cannot stress it enough, you need to face this, and soon."

"It's . . . it's so much harder than you know," she said. "I'm not giving up, I just need more time."

He stood up from his seat. "This case is starting to turn into an international dispute, Maria. Soon, I won't even be able to help you. I received notification from the courthouse in Athens, it seems that Marko has filed for divorce over in Greece. He's claiming that you abandoned them, and that would give him a pretty strong case. It won't help to ignore this, it will just make things harder."

Maria said nothing. She wanted to do something, really she did, but how could she face Marko again? Just the thought of being in the same room frightened her, in the sense that she would not be able to control herself with nothing but furniture and other people between her and him. He had put her through the worst nightmare of her life, she would never forgive him. The emotions she felt when she thought of him scared her, she would not be able to control what she did when she saw him again.

Taking her silence as resignation, Tom sighed. "You are only making it easier for him, Maria. You're practically handing this fight to him on a silver platter. Much like you did Gabriel."

Maria bolted from her chair. His words struck just the wrong nerve. She was almost ready to strike him, so angry he had made her. But she stopped when she saw his eyes. They were concerned, almost sad for her, but his eyes told her he had a lot of sympathy for her situation, like he understood it more than she knew. He was making her face the one thing she blamed herself for, hoping it would rock her from the lull she had fallen into, so that she might feel something, anything. Apparently, it worked like a charm because she felt a stirring passion and fighting spirit swelling within her after so many months of being dead inside.

"You can do this Maria. More than that, you have to. Just remember, you don't have to do it alone. We are all here to support you."

Maria gave his words plenty of consideration. The thought of Marko winning this fight by default filled her with a savage rage. That was not how it was going to be, not if she had any say in it. She would fight to get Gabriel back if it killed her. No matter how long it took, would be back by her side.

"You look like you've had a change of heart," he said.

"Yes, I think I have," Maria said.

"I've found you an international lawyer, someone who can really help you take the fight to Marko. Do you think you'll be ready by the day after tomorrow?"

"Yes, thank you."

"You can save your thanks for when we win."

PART V

TIME HAS NO MEANING

Finally rid of her depression, Maria did all she was able to start the fight for her son. Tom had aided her in getting all the information she needed, and she started by picking up the phone. She contacted this new lawyer to get a feel for what he was like.

As it turned out, the new lawyer, a gentleman by the name of Alastor, was also the lawyer for the Greek Embassy. He confessed that he had already talked about her case with Tom, but he wanted to hear from her what was going on. She told him everything there was to tell about the situation.

Alastor was quiet for a moment upon hearing her story. "It's quite a concern that Marko was able to get a new passport without you present. That's a shoddy job on the Embassy's part. We should be able to get their full cooperation on this, if simply for the fact that they will want to cover up their mistake."

Maria was simultaneously excited and aggravated by that bit of news. It was good that they could expect some help, but the fact that this whole mess could have been prevented if the Embassy had done their job properly really flustered her.

"One more thing, Maria, then I will make a few more calls and we can get our case all together," Alastor said. "Do you have any knowledge of Gabriel's whereabouts?"

"No," Maria said.

"Is there any family in Greece that you could contact that might know?"

Maria started to respond in the negative again, when something clicked in her mind. "I might be able to talk to Ioanna, my mother-in-law."

"Good, then. You do that, find out as much as you can. There might be something we can use."

After she hung up with Alastor, she immediately picked up the phone again to call Ioanna. She realized as she was calling that she never considered calling Ioanna before, mostly because she believed that her mother in law may be involved in Gabriel's abduction. She shook her head vigorously, trying to get that thought out of her head. It was impossible, Ioanna never would have agreed to such a heinous crime, no matter how much she loved her grandson.

But now, Maria needed to know just how bad things were for poor little Gabriel, and maybe Ioanna could help. For all she knew, Marko had the boy locked in his room with bars on the windows, a prisoner in his own home. She needed to know if he was alright; her heart could not bear the thought of him suffering any longer.

Her mother in law was very sensible, and held Marko's ear on many occasions. She might have known where Gabriel was or at least if he was alright.

The phone rang several times. Maria's heart beat harder after each ring, the anxiety bearing down on her. Her mind filled with the images of her son all alone in a dark room, much as she was not long ago, both victims of Marko's malice. It was all Maria could do to keep from screaming.

"Hello?" a voice said in Greek on the other end of the line. It was Ioanna.

"Hello, Ioanna," Maria said, controlling her emotions by a thread. "It's Maria,"

Silence filled the next few seconds. "Hello Maria," Ioanna said reluctantly, "Why are you calling?"

"I need to know," Maria pleaded, "Do you know where my son is?"

"Yes, he is here," Ioanna replied calmingly, "He is playing up in his room."

Maria sighed in relief. Gabriel was somewhere safe, and hopefully he was happy as well. She wanted to talk to him, but worried that Marko might catch him while they were talking, and did not want her boy to be hurt because of her.

"Is Marko there as well?" Maria asked cautiously.

"No, he isn't," Ioanna told her. "He and his band are touring in Yugoslavia. He just showed up with little Gabriel one day and left him here."

Maria had to bite her tongue to stop from yelling. This was a new low for him. Did Marko even care about his son? He had stolen his son away, not so he could have him, but just so Maria could not have him. The sheer wickedness of his behavior made Maria's stomach turn.

Maria tried to calm herself down. After all, at least he had not hurt the boy. "Ioanna," Maria said after she had gotten past her anger, "do you think I could talk with my son?"

Ioanna seemed to hesitate. "Yes, I think it will be alright."

There was a minute of quiet on Ioanna's side, but to Maria it might as well have been an hour. Finally there was a little voice on the other end.

"Hello," said the cheerful voice of little Gabriel.

"Hello," Maria said, tears rolling down her cheeks. "It's your Mama Sou, Gabriel."

"Mama Sou, I miss you," Gabriel said sweetly.

"I miss you too," Maria said, smiling through her tears.

Being able to speak with her son was such a rush. So many memories flew back into her mind when they spoke. Just simple things, like picking him up and holding him tight, holding his hand while they walked to the store, watching the glow in his eyes while she read him a story, and helping him brush his tiny little teeth brought her back to the best times in her life. She etched every second of the phone call into her mind, all of the innocent love she felt scribed into her psyche to remember for all of time. She would never take for granted the time she had on the phone with her son, it was the most precious thing she had now.

After a few more calls, Maria found out why Ioanna seemed so apprehensive in their first conversation since the separation. Apparently when Marko had returned to Greece with Gabriel, he told his mother and sister that Maria was not to be considered a part of the family any longer. They had asked him for a reason, but he would not give them details. All he would say was that she was not to have Gabriel under any circumstances, period, no questions asked.

He received an offer shortly after that for his band to perform in Yugoslavia, where he could potentially earn a lot of money and meet some influential people. He had been working toward such a thing for years, and fully expected it to be the taking off point of his musical career. He would have no time for anything else; he needed to focus on this to make his wildest dreams come true.

Everything else would have to be put on hold. He told his mother to look after Gabriel for him, as if he was her own son. She did, of course, because she loved her grandson dearly.

However, she resented the fact that Maria had let her son go so easily. She felt that anyone who would just leave a darling boy like Gabriel did not deserve his love. He was going to need stronger role models than that in his life.

So it definitely came as a shock to her to find out from Maria that Marko had absconded away with the boy, with a warrant for his arrest in effect if he ever set foot back in America. Maria refrained from speaking her mind, she had no desire at all to tell Ioanna that her son was a wretched person. She had already lost so much when Gabriel Sr. had passed, Maria did not want to hurt her further. She decided that the truth was harmful. It would not bring happiness, and thus was best ignored. So much more important things existed than the nitty-gritty details of a familial kidnapping. She did not want to give such a terrible act any more weight than it actually had, and just talking about it would not help anyone. It was information she wished she never had, and would thus not share any more.

After learning the truth, Ioanna was far more generous in her mood towards Maria. She gave her all the time she could with Gabriel over the phone, perhaps as a way to make up for her son's atrocity. There was nothing else that could have been done until the courts gave their verdict in both countries. Maybe then Maria would be able to see her son and be part of the family once again, but only as the mother of little Gabriel.

However, by the time Ioanna learned the truth, little Gabriel was becoming quite used to his life over in Greece. He was quite content to be with Ioanna and his uncle Stavros, Marko's younger brother. Maria was fine with it; it would only be temporary anyway. There was no court in the world that would side with Marko after her lawyers in Greece received all the details on the case, she would have her son back in just a few months. Both Maria and Ioanna did not want to upset the boy by uprooting him from a stable home again, not when the courts were still out on any decision they might have to change in the future. It was better for him now that he just stayed where he was. Maria was hesitant to admit it, but at least she knew he was safe, and in the hands of someone who loved him.

Still it hurt. She just loved him so much, missing him every moment she had to herself. But the calls were expensive, and she had to cover those calls on her own dime, her parents could not afford the extra charge. She stuck to her schedule, calling whenever she could afford it. Missing him became part of this "new self" she was becoming. This self was empty and lonely, trying to be filled with a child's words to dull a pain that was more than she could stand. But it was all temporary. She had to believe that. It was destined to change someday, she just needed to work toward it and wait. Patience and persistence were not things she had exercised so much until lately. She had to practice them daily now, make them a part of her new self to survive for her son.

The court battle was to be fought on two grounds, in the Boston courtroom where Maria was, and over in Athens. Hearings in one courtroom needed to be brought to the other for reference, so going was very slow. Neither court actually recognized the progress in the other, but the attorneys needed the rulings to formulate their strategies and support their cases.

During the court proceedings, Maria was hungry for hope. She had never had to endure so much unpleasantness all at once. The tedious legal battles were slowly but surely whittling away her normally positive and spirited way of looking at life. She had to sit quietly while she was told that people she never met told lies about her, people it was clear Marko had paid to lie. Because of the standing warrant for his arrest, Marko was never there, and that was fine with her. If she never saw him again, she could die happy.

Thankfully, she did not have to deal with all that unpleasantness alone. Her mother had agreed to help, even if it was just to be there by her side during it all. Whenever she noticed Maria was upset, she would hold her hand, whispering, "You can do this. You are strong. I know you can do this." Maria would squeeze her hand back, and just feel her mother's strength empowering her through some invisible connection. It gave her confidence, something she desperately needed in this dark time.

Her father supported her in actions, but emotionally he seemingly had washed his hands of the entire affair, but Maria knew that her mother talked with him about it and kept him updated. Somehow, he was just as affected as Maria about the whole ordeal; he just managed to hide it better. He had failed to protect her from this nightmare, so he tried to stay out of it in case he made it worse.

For the most part, the arguments and action that happened in the Boston courtroom were about getting continuances. Tom tried very hard to get a resolution for this situation every time, and Marko's lawyer always had some reason or another that it be allowed, stalling the progress of the battle even further.

On the few occasions there was any kind of actual debate on her case, Marko's lawyer tried to bring up evidence of her being negligent or otherwise unfit to be a mother. However, Tom was an incredible researcher and debater. Each time Marko's lawyer brought up some incident of Maria's neglect, Alastor had a rebuttal and evidence to prove him wrong. If it had not been for his skill and foresight, Maria might have given up long ago. Between Alastor, Tom, and her mother, she felt each session was much more bearable.

Starved as she was for the presence of her son, she called Ioanna as often as she could to talk to him. She could not call every day, her parent's phone bill was high enough as it was. But once a week or so, between work and court, she tried to make a short call to Ioanna. Not every call was worth it; sometimes Gabriel would be away or asleep, but for every such call she had three others that made her hold on to hope, giving her peace of mind and the will to carry on.

At times Ioanna was reluctant, but usually Maria was allowed to have contact with her son. Those conversations with Gabriel were little candles in a long hallway of darkness, the only way for her to get through it were to look forward to the tiny glowing lights, few and far between though they were. She felt as though each one was brighter than the last, and that soon these little lights would all glow as one at the end of the very long tunnel.

It was a hard life, fighting for her beloved son almost every day. There was always a phone call, a letter from the court, notification from her lawyers, or copies of documents from Greece to deal with, but Maria held her faith. Good things come to those with patience, she thought, and patience was an old friend now. The truth of things would show in the end, as long as she concentrated and made sure not to leave anything out. In the end, she would get her justice and her son. All this would be worth it, and she would not have to fight anymore for what was already hers.

One day, about a year and a half after her court battle began, she called up Ioanna. She needed very much just to hear Gabriel's voice, and it had been some time since she had talked to him anyway. She had not been able to call, by some series of circumstances, for quite a while, and she longed for the drug of his sweet voice. The past few times he had been out or asleep, so nearly a month had elapsed since they talked.

"Hello," came Ioanna's voice over the phone.

"Hello Ioanna," Maria said. "Is it okay if I talk to Gabriel?"

"No, Maria," Ioanna said, her voice much quieter, and touched with emotion.

Maria paused for a moment, shocked. A draining realization hit her then: had Marko's lies gotten to her? "Ioanna, if this is about something Marko said . . ."

"No, it wasn't what he said to me," Ioanna replied. Maria was thankful at first; Ioanna, along with Maria's sister in law Lysa, had always been a silent supporter of her side of things, even though Marko was her son.

At least Maria believed it was so. They had never stood up to Marko on her behalf, but neither did they impede Maria's access to Gabriel. The fact that they did not want to stop her from fighting this battle meant so very much to her, so very validating in a sublime fashion. It did not matter that they did not fight Marko themselves, it was not their fight. The fact that they supported her, even silently, was the most substantial thing they could do for her from where they were. It was only due to her love that Maria was able to feel justified in her fight.

"Then what is it?" Maria asked, her dread overcome by her curiosity.

"Marko came back from abroad a few weeks ago," Ioanna explained. "little Gabriel, thinking that you were coming with his father, asked him where you were and when his Mama Sou was coming back."

"That's good!" Maria said, brightening up a little. Even her little baby boy must have known something was wrong to ask such questions.

"Maria, you can't call here anymore," Ioanna said strongly, but her voice trailed off. There was a pause, and then she said, "Marko told him that you were dead and never coming back."

Maria lost her breath. This was too much for her to handle. Marko's capacity for cruelness had reached a new low. It was one thing to keep hurting Maria, but how could he just say something so horrible to Gabriel?

"Please Ioanna," she pleaded. "Let me tell him the truth!"

"Marko is still here in Greece," Ioanna said quietly. "I don't think his trip went well, he was very angry with me. This is the last time we talk, Maria. I am so sorry."

"I just want to talk to him."

"Goodbye, Maria," she said, and before hanging up, she whispered, "Good luck."

Maria slowly lowered the receiver, staring at it in shock. Her hand seemed to move in slow motion as she hung up the phone, processing what had just taken place. Her son thought she was dead now. It was practically the worst scenario she could have imagined. No, it was the worst. She literally could not have imagined a worse fate, outside of actual death.

But it did not matter. She still had the court battle. If she won, she would get her divorce and go to Greece, and then Marko would have no choice but to give Gabriel back to her. All she had to do was keep at it. Patience, piety, and persistence would win the fight, time was the obstacle more than anything else. Just keep going to court, it would all be over soon.

But it was not over soon; not at all. Marko's lawyer repeatedly requested continuances, trying to stall the court case even further. Unless Maria's side was able to give a good reason why the continuance could not be granted, it was usually allowed. Other times, it was Maria's lawyers that requested the continuance, usually to wait for something beneficial to come out of the court case in Athens. The time between sessions was often quite a long period, sometimes as long as six months.

She eventually realized that with every extension, every wait, little Gabriel went on believing that his mother was dead. He would continue to grow and move on, accepting that horrible lie as the truth. Marko had made it almost impossible for her to ever even see her son again. If she did see him now, how devastated would the shock be to her poor son?

But it continued. Six months of working and waiting, almost every time there was a continuance. Maria's life trudged on regardless of her luck in court, six months at a time. She had saved up enough working to get herself a car of her own, a used old car, but it was still a little bit more independence. Holidays came and went like little storms in her life, bringing a maelstrom of family and joy for a time, and leaving as quickly as they came. Everyone that knew what was going on was very supportive of her, and she was always grateful to have anyone on her side.

She needed to concentrate now, to focus on something positive, something within her power to control. That was when she decided to attend college. It was for her future, and her son's future. After all, she *would* get him back someday, and she needed to be the best role model she could be for him. Northeastern University was near her work, and she had time in the evening to study. Her decision made, she felt much better. There was a glimmer of anticipation in her future, the possibility of some measure of excitement and happiness.

Still she felt guilty for feeling happy, an inevitable guilt that followed her through her life. She was not with her son yet, how could she possibly be happy yet? The emotional teeter totter she lived day to day was just something she grew used to after time.

It was not until years later that she realized how easily she had moved on from her despair and disruption. It had been five years since Gabriel had been taken away, yet here she was, living her life and doing what she must, carrying on in the shadow of a broken little family. Gabriel was now almost nine years old; it was possible that he did not even remember her. She still fought for her son whenever there was a court date, but there was so much more to her life than that. The longer this phase of her life lasted, the more she settled in to the new self. This self was all about just that, the self. It was self reliant, self sustainable. But also it was very selfish, hoarding trust and love from anyone but those she deemed worthy, and that list was small indeed.

Little by little, she was stepping away from her tragedy, making it a distant point on the horizon of her life. Sometimes she would look back and it would seem much closer, but like with much else in her life now, she just pushed it away. She learned to push harder every time, and the pain eventually became a speck that she barely recognized.

How must things have changed for Gabriel, now? His life must be so different from when she last saw him. Who were his friends? Was he happy? How was his schooling going? Was he even in school? What had it been like for him to lose his first tooth? What kind of games did he play, books had he read, songs did he sing? His life was just one big question to Maria now. Perhaps the most troubling question of all was the one she desperately tried to avoid in her mind: did her son even remember her now?

In a way, she was almost thankful that Gabriel thought she was dead. She did not want to think of him going through the anguish that she felt; he would be going through everything that she was being forced to suffer, and she would not have wished that on anyone. She often asked herself if she could take him away from everything he knew, throw away his life on a whim just to drag him back with her. She tried not to think too much on this, the fight was already being fought. It wore on her, though, making her confused and hesitant. She honestly did not know what she would do if she got a favorable verdict. Would she — could she — bring him back?

Time continued to pass, in the quaintly curious way it always does. Every time the court convened, it seemed it was just as quickly adjourned under the pretense of another continuance. Maria was beginning to feel it would never end. Was all this time, all this effort, just to keep her from getting a simple divorce? It made no sense for it to take so long, not when her case was so obviously one sided. It had been years since Marko's lawyer had produced any kind of relevant evidence, why was this allowed to continue?

These thoughts began to mount as her next court date approached. How many more times would she have to do this before it was all over? Would she have to keep doing this for as long as she lived? She needed this to stop; it could not go on forever. But how could she stop it? She had to rely on her lawyers to get this done, but she knew they were doing all they could within the bounds of their positions.

Her heart strained silently as she entered the courtroom that day. Everyone did the things they always did, but it was all so painfully familiar to her this time. Tom shuffled his notes, Alastor cleared his throat as though preparing for a speech, her mother hummed to herself, and Marko's lawyer folded his hands calmly over his briefcase.

The judge then came in, and upon taking his seat looked upon them all with a degree of dismay, as though he was just as fed up with it all as Maria was. They began, reciting relevant facts from the last hearing in Athens, which was to say not much. Almost immediately after, Marko's lawyer stood and asked for a continuance. The judge sighed and raised his gavel, about to grant it.

Enough. It was enough now. It could not continue this way. She could never see her son again anyway, he would be torn apart by the confusion and agony this would cause him. Why was she still fighting? What was she fighting for, if not her son?

"No! Not again!" she said, almost unaware that the words were leaving her mouth. Maria's hands began to shake, and her mother tried to console her. She tried to stifle a sob, but tears were already coming down. It was too much to bear. She did not care what everyone thought of her, she had her fill of this place and wanted it to be over with.

The judge paused for a moment, glancing at Marko's lawyer and then at Maria's lawyers. He then looked to her and said, "Young lady, do you have something you want to say?"

Maria nodded, and the judge asked her to come up to the stand. He ordered the bailiff to give her a box of tissues, then swore her in, and the judge asked her what was really going on. So Maria answered the judge's questions, explained everything as best she could, as concisely as possible, from her point of view. It was a great relief to actually explain everything like this, it was almost therapeutic.

After hearing her story, the judge looked across the courtroom to Marko's lawyer, who looked slightly concerned. "Do you still want your continuance?" he said.

"No, your honor," he said.

"Your client has thirty days to show up in this court, or produce some evidence or witness to the contrary, or I shall grant this poor woman her divorce."

"Yes, your honor. Understood."

Maria was lead down from the stand and she took her seat once more. Alastor looked pleasantly surprised, and Tom seemed to be hiding a satisfied smirk. Her mother remained quietly excited, mirroring Maria's own state of mind.

After court was adjourned and just as Maria and her mother were leaving, she was approached by Marko's lawyer.

"Ma'am, I just wanted to say good luck."

"Really?" she said, rather perplexed.

"I never met your husband, and never knew the whole story. He just sent me money in an envelope to keep the case going, and a note just saying to deny you the divorce." He shook her hand. "I really hope you get your son back."

Maria was overjoyed. This whole ordeal was coming to an end, finally. All of what happened—Marko's cruelty, the kidnapping, the lie he told to Gabriel—meant nothing now; it was all in the past.

However, it was not over yet. She still had so many decisions to make, very difficult, life changing decisions, choices that would affect her and her son very deeply. She doubted that she could make such important decisions. She had been acting so selfishly lately, could she still make the best choice for both of them? Should she follow her heart, or her mind? Should she tell her son she was still alive, or save him the shock and let him believe otherwise?

It was far from over, things would not be okay yet.

About a month later, Tom came to the house to see her. He did not look like he brought good news.

"Tom? Did Marko show up?" Maria asked, terrified.

"No," he replied. "In fact, you've won. The judge awarded you the divorce and full custody of your son this morning."

"But that's amazing news!" Maria said. "We won, didn't we?"

"Yes, but that's not the important part," he explained. "Even though you won the case and have sole custody, you aren't an American citizen. The court cannot actually act on the decision unless Marko decides to bring him back for some reason. I even tried going to the Portuguese Embassy to get them to help, but they refused to get involved in the situation. I'm so sorry, Maria."

Maria sighed. "It's alright. We did it, we won. It's okay now."

"But your son . . . ?"

"He's safe with his grandmother. That's all that matters." It was that simple, all her conflict disappeared with nine little words. She was certain this decision was right, she would not look back. Maybe she would see him in the future, but now it was fine.

Maria gave Tom a hug. "Thank you again for everything."

Tom gave her a profound look. "You've been through so much, this is not fair for you at all. I can't do anything more, but I bet one day God will reward you, in His own way. Just you wait and see."

"I bet he will," Maria said, smiling. "I'm pretty good at waiting now."

Maria's life did not change much at first. But as time passed and life came to her, she let life come. Her studies had started, slowly at first as evening classes were, but it allowed her to research several of the university's majors. She was compelled by the idea of computer science, and decided to declare her major and start to learn about programming. Soon she discovered she had a talent for it, in both systems analysis and later in software engineering.

There were no trust issues to be had in Computer Science. She kept minimal contact with others, the machines were fairly predictable, and could mostly be trusted. She fit very well into the workforce of the world of computers, she was able to work alone as an individual contributor and still be a part of a bigger project, which matched perfectly with how she interacted with others. She made amends with the family Marko had broken apart, salvaging everything she could from the old conflicts around the kidnapping. The only regret she came away with was that they had lost so much time.

♑ ♓ ♑ ♓ ♑ ♓ ♑ ♓ ♑ ♓ ♑ ♓

Years passed, and everything seemed to change. She eventually met and fell in love with a man named Terry, with whom she married—an arrangement which she did not enter into easily—and had three wonderful sons. She was able to let herself love again, albeit slowly and steadily, and it felt so good. Shadows of her past crept in from time to time. Every milestone, birthday, and life situation, regardless of what it was, brought back agonizing memories of her old life, but she endured the pain stoically. The pain meant something, it reminded her of Gabriel. Her first son would always have a place in her heart.

One morning, just before noon, she sat at home, working on the computer, when her phone rang. She picked up, saying, "Hello?"

"Hello Maria," her mother said on the other line. Her voice was restrained and quiet, as though she was hesitant. For a moment Maria wondered if something bad had happened. "How are you doing today?"

"I'm fine, I'm just working . . ." she started to reply, but was cut off by her mother.

"You need to come by the house," she said harshly in a low tone. "Be here by two o'clock tomorrow, it's very important."

Something about her tone was not right. Her mother could be forceful sometimes, but never outright told her she had to come to the house. Maria asked her what happened, if she was ill, if someone was hurt, but only got silence in return. Moments where her mother was silent worried Maria the most. Finally, her mother spoke up in a breaking, tearful voice.

"Gabriel called."

Maria's heart skipped a beat. Did she hear her mother right, or was her mind playing tricks on her? "What did you say?"

"He called me, Maria! I knew he would someday!" Her mother was practically in hysterics. "I never moved from this house, because one day I knew he would try to call us again! I told him you lived far away, but would be here when he called back tomorrow!"

Maria's stunned silence spoke volumes of how unable she was to process this information. She knew the words her mother was saying made sense; they were in the correct order, but she was unable to understand them.

"Didn't you hear me? Gabriel is back, you can talk to him tomorrow!"

"Oh my God . . ." And just like that, everything that happened between the day he was kidnapped and that moment was gone. She was right back in that moment, and all of the emotion returned in full force. She could not respond at all, only repeat "oh my God" several times. Her baby boy had called looking for her, she would be able to talk to him tomorrow.

"Maria, are you okay?"

She snapped out of it, getting a grasp on her mind long enough to put words together. "Oh mom, thank you so much! I'll be there tomorrow morning!"

The next day she was on her way just before eleven o'clock, excited and apprehensive all at once. After all this time, she had the chance to speak to her son again. That was the most amazing, unbelievable thing she could have imagined. But she had so many worries about what he might have thought about her. He beat her to it, after all. She planned on waiting until he was eighteen to even try to contact him. Maybe he was angry at her for not trying to contact him sooner, maybe he thought she forgot about him. Maybe he had moved on, and did not want her in his life. But then why would he call?

When she got to the house, she realized how many memories from back then still lingered. Oh, there were bad ones from when she was depressed, sure. But there were good ones from before all that had happened. She remembered the time she had first visited her parents after marrying Marko, when Gabriel was still just a baby. They had recently moved and had not updated Maria with their new address yet. She remembered how frightened she had been when she found out her parents address was wrong. She felt alone and disconnected, coming home from a far off country to find they had left the home she had always known. It did not take them long to find them, but when they did, she was so relieved, just happy to share her new family and her old one that the fear she felt before no longer mattered.

She never guessed she would have experienced these feelings twice in one lifetime.

She spent the time until Gabriel called talking with her mother, rehashing the past, and all that had happened since then. It was only then talking with her that Maria realized how much her mother had helped her along during her hardest times. It was because of her that Maria got a job, the job that made her feel like she could be useful again. It was because she tricked Maria into getting driving lessons that she was able to become more independent. She stood by Maria even when she did not entirely agree with her, back when she was first getting her divorce. If it had not been for her stubborn love and devotion, Maria might have given up long before she even lost Gabriel.

In a moment of self reflection, she realized she was raising her boys the same way as her mother, with the same kind of steadfast devotion and care. It struck her that Gabriel had likely not received that kind of attention, and that alone nearly broke Maria again.

For once in a long time, she felt regret. She did not have to let him grow up without a mother, but she left him with practically only his grandmother. Was that supposed to have been easier for him? For thirteen years, she had not once thought to contact him, because of some arbitrary notion that it would have been more difficult for him somehow. All she could hope for now was that Ioanna had loved him enough not to let Marko's influence spread to her baby boy.

Two o'clock approached, and Gabriel had not called. A few minutes later, he still had not called. Maria thought some very distressing thoughts, things that were not realistic or even plausible, but still she thought them. The longer she waited the more upsetting these fantasies became, and her anxieties about Gabriel not wanting her or changing his mind started to become more feasible.

The phone finally rang, and before the first ring had even ended, Maria had picked up the phone. "Hello?"

". . . Hello, is this . . . is this Maria?"

The voice was not one Maria had heard before. It was mature and smooth, but gentle and sweet. She smiled like she never smiled before; she was sure this was her son.

The conversation was stilted and awkward to start, neither of them knew what to say. Gabriel spoke haltingly, as though he was not used to speaking English, so she kept her words simple and slow. He must have sensed her apprehension, because he was very deliberate and careful about what he said.

Maria finally just said what she wanted to say the whole time. "I've really missed you. I think about you all the time, you know. I just wish I could have shared more with you. Whenever I went places or did things I enjoyed, I always wondered if you would have liked it too."

"Really?" he said. "I think about that too."

From there, the conversation really opened up. They talked about things they had done and seen since then, and all the little things that had gone on in their lives. Deep inside Maria, her heart was rejoicing. This was how things were supposed to be, a mother and son catching up over times lost.

She asked him how he found out she was still alive. He explained to her that her sister-in-law Lysa, who had silently supported Maria's side of things, had kept his other grandmother's phone number, just in case. While Ioanna and Gabriel were visiting her, they were talking about Maria when Gabriel walked in the room. They both went silent simultaneously, and he looked at them as though he had discovered something.

"She's still alive, isn't she?" he asked, daring to be hopeful.

Lysa, unable to lie about it anymore, nodded and told him to wait for a moment. She got up from her chair and left the room coming back moments later and gave him a small piece of paper with the phone number on it, just saying, "I knew one day you would want this."

It took a few days for Gabriel to let it all sink in, but as soon as he was ready he made the call.

"Mama Sou"

Their delightful conversation went on for some time. Eventually the subject came up of her coming to visit him in Greece. It absolutely had to happen and soon, Maria felt it deep down. She promised to call him back the next day with details, and after she hung up with him she realized that she did not have the money to afford a trip like that. Their family was young, expenses were high, and there was little extra to spare.

She told her mother, and they spent a little time trying to figure out a way they could get the money they would need in time. When they had exhausted all of their ideas, Maria suggested she tried giving her brother Roy a call.

Maria's mother initially balked at the idea, but at this point they could not find any other option in the time frame she had. Her brother was rather well off, but he distanced himself from the rest of the family. Once in a while he would call their mother, but he was not very close to anyone at all. Maria had fond memories of playing with him when they were children, but now she was not very happy about the idea of asking him for anything. Still, she was ready to do anything to make this trip happen. With no other option available, she picked up the phone and called him at work.

His secretary answered, and asked for her name. Maria told her who she was, and was promptly put on hold. A minute later, her brother picked up. "Hello, Maria."

"Hello Roy, how are you?"

"Are mom and dad okay?" he asked.

"Yes, they're fine."

"Why did you call then?"

This was why Maria did not like to talk to him. His cold attitude repelled her worse than outright cruelty ever could. He always seemed to think the rest of the family beneath him, and spoke to them as though they wasted his time with every breath. She knew there was love beneath the cold surface, but something had changed him that made him feel the need to be so cold. She knew now what that was like, having been changed in a similar way. She still loved him, of course, but his demeanor made him hard to approach.

She decided to be as straightforward as he was, he would appreciate that. "I just got a call from Gabriel. I want to go visit him in Greece but I don't have the money, I wanted to know if I could borrow some."

"Would three thousand be enough for the trip?" His voice was quieter and warmer somehow.

Maria blinked in startled amazement. "Yes, that would be more than enough."

"A pittance to share for something so important," he said, voice still softer. "I'll overnight it to you. Was there anything else?" He seemed uncomfortable asking, as though he realized how much he was showing his vulnerability in doing so.

Maria was shocked and sad. She regretted their distance now, and wished very dearly they had a better relationship. Tears of conflicting emotion ran down her cheeks while she tried to get herself to say anything.

After a few moments of silence, Roy said, in a much kinder tone, "How is Gabriel?"

Maria's smile beamed through her tears. "He's doing very well."

They talked for a little while longer, about the things Maria just talked about with Gabriel, and a little about the plans for the trip. She had not realized how much this debacle had affected him, but he had been genuinely sympathetic to her situation. She simply figured he did not care, just as coldly as he seemed to be, but now it was clear that he certainly cared, enough that he was willing to make a massive investment just for her to see her son again. Maria must have thanked him three more times before they said goodbye and hung up. She would never forget this unbelievable gesture of kindness on her brother's part. Never.

Maria made her arrangements immediately. She called Terry to confirm the plans they had already talked about, and then called to book her flight. She would leave in a few days. In just a few days, she would be able to see the son she had longed to see for almost thirteen years.

"Mama Sou"

Gabriel at 16 years of age

♑♓♑♓♑♓♑♓♑♓♑♓

PART VI

REUNION

Maria had taken this trip many times, back when she and Marko were bouncing between homes. But this trip dragged on where she remembered it not being so arduous. She wanted to relax and stop thinking, but found herself particularly vulnerable to giddiness. The anticipation was making her stomach churn and her as tense as a wire. When Maria arrived in Greece, she was greeted by a young man, handsome and charming, who held up a sign with her name on it. She knew it was Gabriel right away. She could not help but admire what a fine young man he had grown up to be. She worried about how he had grown internally, what virtues he held, how caring he was. He looked very mature for being only sixteen, but she knew what he had gone through, and that would make anyone grow up quickly. That thought saddened her.

She wanted to tell him so much now that she was there with him. On one hand, she wanted to let him know how much she missed him, about all the hardships she went through to try and get him back. But on the other hand, she did not want to burden him with any more pain. With him right there in front of her, there were no words worth saying. Instead she hugged him tight, just happy to be there with him after so much time away.

He brought her to the hotel, so she could unpack and rest a little from her trip, but then took her right back out into Athens. They went out to eat at a fantastic little restaurant, then spent the evening at one of the many jam packed nightclubs, listening to an amazing band and having a grand old time. Gabriel took her out to the nightclub's veranda to sit at one of the tables where they could see the Acropolis, lit up with colored lights. They made the whole place seem closer, and it was even more magnificent when the lights changed color, cascading with the whole spectrum as a story was being told to the tourists watching below.

They were together for every evening of her trip. She could not ask for more than that. Every night it was a new place, just as bustling as the last, but the experience was just as wonderful, just because she was sharing it with her son. They could have spent the time in a fast food place and she would have been just as enthralled. Every second was a blessing, and not a single moment was wasted.

One night though, was very different. Gabriel took her to an outdoor theater, where he was the lead role in a summer stock production of Orpheus that had a contemporary twist to it. She was surprised to learn that he was acting at this level at such a young age, but was amazed at how well he performed. She remembered Orpheus as a tragedy, but the players presented it in a comedic fashion. The whole audience was kept laughing, so splendid was the performance.

When it was all done, Maria went to congratulate Gabriel on such good job. He told her that thanks to this play, he had an opportunity coming very soon to get a part on a daily Greek soap opera with one of the most famous actresses in Greece. His excitement shone through, it was very clear that he was passionate about performing. Maria had witnessed for herself how talented he was; there was no doubt in her mind he could go places.

Not the entire trip was good times. One day Maria got a message from the front desk of the hotel, saying there was a gentleman there to see her. She had instructed them to not give out her room number and inform her when she got a visitor. She felt dread deep down something told her this was not someone she wanted to talk to. She told them not to tell him her room number, but she would talk to them over the phone. Her suspicions proved true, it was Marko's voice she heard over the phone.

"Can I come see you?" he asked.

"You cannot," she told him firmly.

"Why not?"

Maria fumed for a moment. How dare he even say that! She could not even begin to comprehend all the things that were wrong with him asking her that question. She needed to stop this before anything terrible could come out of it. Her time here with Gabriel was precious, and she would not allow Marko to ruin it in any way.

It was time for her to tell Marko something she had always wanted to say to him.

"Why would you want to see me? You clearly don't want anything to do with me, seeing as you took my son from me when he was less than three years old. You told him that I was dead, you told your family to support that lie. You made me and Gabriel go through such agony and loss, and *now* you want to see me?"

"But I . . ."

"No, Marko. I don't want you or need you anymore. No, I stand corrected, I *never* needed you. Compared to the rest of my life, you have been the most insignificant creature I've had the misfortune of being involved with. I don't want to see you again. And I mean *ever* again. There is no reason for you to be here, and no reason for me to see you. Get out and go on your way."

And just like that, she never heard from Marko again.

Later, when she saw Gabriel again, she felt so relieved. He could have become like Marko after spending so much time with him, but she realized later that would never have happened. She knew early on that her son was going to become a good person. Her son, who when he was very little, grabbed his father's leg and told him not to fight with her, the little boy who would clutch at her legs and call her "mama-sou," was a gentle soul who was filled with love.

During that same week, she found out that Gabriel did inherit one trait from his father: the ability to sing. Even better, his talent for it vastly surpassed his father's. Hearing him sing made Maria ever so slightly prideful, that her son, at such a young and tender age, could already outdo his father at the one thing he thought he could do well.

Near the end of her ten day stay in Greece, Gabriel invited her to have dinner with Ioanna and her family. He did not say as much, but it was clear that this was very important to Gabriel. Maria reluctantly agreed, providing that Marko would not be there. Gabriel promised her that he definitely would not be invited; he was currently not on speaking terms with his father either. She was somewhat apprehensive of seeing familiar faces again, but if that's what Gabriel wanted her to do, she would do her best.

Coming into the room and seeing everyone there brought forth a well of once subdued emotions in Maria. These people had perpetuated the lie of her death, after all, keeping her from seeing her son for over a decade. The thought made her wish she never agreed to come, and stayed away from the family for the rest of her life.

But as the night went on, and she got to know familiar people all over again, she put together that many of them did not even know the truth of the matter until long after what had happened. Marko said she was dead; there was no reason to doubt him. Ioanna was the only person who knew the whole truth from the beginning. She just wanted to protect Gabriel, and keep the family together. In their position, Maria realized she would have done much the same.

At one point, Lysa caught her alone and tried to apologize for the whole thing, but Maria stopped her. She told her, "Don't worry about it. I understand what was going on, what you were told, the whole situation. It's all in the past now. There's so much more to look forward to now, let's not waste any energy dredging up the past. We can't change it, it's best to move on and focus on the future, and on Gabriel's happiness."

Lysa nodded her understanding. "Life has made you wise, Maria. I'm glad to see you again."

The dinner went wonderfully, with lots of stories, food and drink, and catching up. Maria had truly missed them since she was gone, but had not felt it truly until now. Even though she was divorced from Marko, these people still treated her like she was a long lost relative, and in a way she was.

Somewhere during the meal, the topic of discussion turned to Gabriel's studies, a topic which he apparently did not like to discuss. It turned out that Gabriel wanted to go into acting and singing as a full time career, but certain members of the family thought that was too impractical. Maria could not blame them, seeing the way that Marko turned out. They simply did not want Gabriel to be another starving artist. His father had worn that mantle for far too long, and it would be painful for them to watch Gabriel follow in those ill-fated footsteps. The problem was they had no other real role model for him.

It turned out that he had been studying electronics in school and had the chance to go to university for it immediately. But Gabriel was adamant that he could do well as a performer, and he had a great opportunity lined up, the one he had told Maria about after the play. He had the attention of some very influential people, and if he did well he could have a shot at being famous.

This debate continued for some time, and Maria held her peace until Lysa asked her what she thought. All eyes were on her for that moment, including Gabriel. After keeping in mind all she had learned, she decided what to say.

"Gabriel," she started, "you must know that everyone here just wants what's best for you. That is why they want you to finish school, it could be so important!"

Gabriel looked somewhat disappointed in her words, but she kept going. "But there's no saying you can't do both, you know! It might not be easy for a while, but you most certainly can go to school and keep up your performing. Just think how nice it would be to have that diploma, all the while working on your performing career. There is nothing stopping you from having all you want. The only thing that can stop you is you. I just know that whatever you decide to do, you will have our support."

His smile was the greatest reward Maria could ask for.

Shortly after that trip, Gabriel proceeded to show everyone what he could do when it came to music and composing, what he could accomplish with his passion for music. Several of his recordings went Gold and some others went Platinum, he became a very popular artist in Greece, Europe, and many other countries.

Maria received a call by a local TV station and invited to surprise him "on-air" during an upcoming interview. She reluctantly agreed, and immediately called Ioanna to find out her opinion on the matter. Maria didn't want to have this "surprise" be an unwanted one and desperately needed to get Ioanna's view of it.

To Maria's surprise, she was quite excited. "That's wonderful! I'm also invited to speak at this interview. It would be a good surprise for Gabriel to hear your voice again and show his fans a connection to his mother." Ioanna told her. Maria felt so much relief after she heard that.

"Thank you Ioanna. I will look forward to the call and I hope I will make my son happy with my answers." She said. They said their goodbyes and hung up. The call was short, but Ioanna was genuinely happy to know that Maria was asked and was part of the surprise for Gabriel. Her short bursts of laughter reassured Maria that she was!

The call went well. Gabriel was surprised when the hostess of the show announced that Maria was on the phone. After about 4-5 questions, the call was over and Maria wished so strongly that she had been there in person, watching his son receive this surprise — which also included an award for his musical accomplishments. She couldn't be happier.

After that she, and her entire family, had gone to see Gabriel during several of his tours through Boston and New York. They were all treated like stars, which made Maria and Terry's sons, Gabriel's half-brothers, so excited to be there and receive such attention from the fans and the support staff, not to mention each got a backstage pass. All three were in their early teens, and were definitely star-stuck. They had never been backstage at any event! It was an experience they will remember always.

Many events followed, but one in particular hit Maria with such a force and made her realize, truly, what her son had accomplished. She had been invited by another TV Station to appear, again as a surprise, in a TV show where Gabriel was being honored and interviewed for his many accomplishments and contribution to music in Greece.

The TV station took care of her trip and accommodations in Athens. But it was not during the show or at the studio that Maria had that deep emotional experience that she would never forget, it was in her hotel room. She had just checked in and was unpacking. She turned on the TV and felt like listening to some music. She tuned into MTV, but this was European MTV. Some of the music she was not very familiar with, but it was very good. So, she continued to unpack and suddenly she heard a familiar song, sang by her son, playing on MTV. She stopped what she was doing, completely immobile, trying to process what she was hearing coming out of the TV that was tuned into a major music station that people were watching all over Europe and beyond, and her son was the musician singing it. It was his composition, his arrangement, his lyrics, his video, *his song*. Her mind was blown away, and at the same time humility set in. Finally, gratitude — so overwhelming that it made her cry. All she could say between sobs was "Thank you. Thank you for giving him so much to try to fill the void created many years ago!"

This is not the end of our story, just a temporary interruption to a beautiful beginning.

Epilogue

The following are some personal words that Maria herself wanted me to add. Instead of trying to rewrite it, here is the entirety of her text, with no editing. T.C.

Could some things have been done differently? Most likely so. I could have been less strong-minded and independent. I could have bitten my tongue and let indiscretions and betrayal be. I could have been happy to have a husband that had received an inheritance that could eventually give me all my life's desires. I could have not stopped at the attorney's office and start divorce proceedings. I could have denied Marko the privilege to take Gabriel to the circus. I could have . . . . I could . . . . I . . . . Too many variables! Too many options! All these led to my worst memories!

Now I find myself with a son that doesn't know me and a son that I really don't know. I wasn't there to take care of him when he was sick as a little boy and nurse him back to health. I wasn't able to be there on his first day of school and wave good bye, or pick him up after school was over. I wasn't able to be the "tooth fairy" and leave a coin under his pillow in exchange for his tiny tooth. I wasn't able to hear about how his day went at school, who his friends were, who he had a crush on. I wasn't able to hug him tight and rock him back to sleep when he had a nightmare. I wasn't able to read to him, or help him learn how to read.

I wasn't able to create his first Halloween costume, or put make up on him to make him look like a pirate, or hold his hand while going door to door to trick-or-treat. I wasn't there to go shopping with him, get him the clothes that were "cool" to wear to school, or purchase for him the games his school friends wish they had. I wasn't there to fulfill his Christmas lists; to see his face full of wonder when opening the gifts he had wished for on Christmas morning. I wasn't there to sing him "Happy Birthday", help him blow out his candles, bake him his favorite cake, and give him his most desirable gift.

I wasn't able to wait up for him and find out if he had a good time or a bad time on his first date. I wasn't there to explain to him how to be with a girl—what to do, what to say, what is right and what is wrong to feel towards a girl. I wasn't there to tell him about love. To explain how it feels. What it makes you do. How to respect a girl and how to respect yourself. I wasn't there to teach him about loyalty, dignity, caring, and responsibility. I wasn't able to give him a ride to work, or to pick him up when he was done. I wasn't there to show him by example . . . I wasn't there to *be* an example!

Regrets have nothing to do with how I feel. Regrets will not change anything. Regrets are not useful and are dark spaces you cannot come back from. Everything that I have done has been my choice, whether or not it was a good choice, it was mine and I had a reason to make that choice. I know there are consequences to every choice we make and I have accepted them. I believe I have learned by each and every one of my decisions. So, they were not made in vain . . . there was a lesson to be learned, and by now I have learned many, many lessons.

There has been much that has transpired since Gabriel and I found each other again . . . His rise to national and international stardom in the music world. Priceless memories created during my trips to meet with him at several locations on his tours through New England and my trips to Greece. The wonderful times we had, however few, during the occasions we were able to be together and talk, learn about each other, discover our likes and dislikes; our relationship since then and during his extremely busy music career has been a challenge that we are still struggling to overcome. And, most importantly, how the past has affected us both in the present . . . . Our lives, lived separately but always with each other in mind—but that's a story for another day.

The only thing left to say is that I have done my best. I don't take shortcuts, but I also don't waste time. I like to get to the point and cut through all that is unnecessary. I do what, in my mind, is the right thing to do. I am at peace right now. I feel very lucky to have four wonderful sons, each very special in his own way, and each makes me very, very proud to be a mother. That is the greatest feeling in life—and I feel it times four! There is a reason for everything—and someday I will find out what has been the reason for losing my oldest son so many years ago.

When something bad happens in life, you have three choices. You can either let it define you, let it destroy you, or you can let it strengthen you. This third one, in my mind, is the hardest choice to make, but the only one I would consider. This was definitely not the end of our story. There is a lot more to tell, but that is a story for another day. I hope that you will be bold enough to use your voice, brave enough to listen to your heart, and strong enough to live the life you've always imagined.

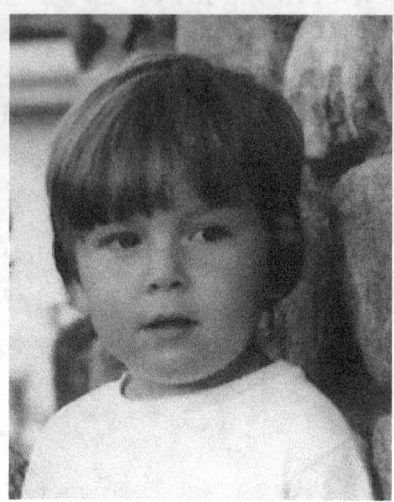

Maria   Gabriel at 2 and a half years of age

Maria and Gabriel days before he was taken

www.ingramcontent.com/pod-product-compliance
Lightning Source LLC
Chambersburg PA
CBHW052100070526
44584CB00017B/2266